CARIAN INSCRIPTIONS
FROM NORTH SAQQÂRA
AND BUHEN

EXCAVATIONS AT NORTH SAQQÂRA

DIRECTED BY W. B. EMERY

DOCUMENTARY SERIES

UNDER THE GENERAL DIRECTION OF H. S. SMITH

3. Olivier Masson, *Carian Inscriptions
from North Saqqâra and Buhen*

———

NOTE. The excavations of the Egypt Exploration Society in
the Sacred Animal Necropolis at North Saqqâra, initiated by
the late Professor W. B. Emery in 1964, yielded a great many
documents written in different scripts and languages. The
various groups of documents, prepared for publication by
many scholars, will appear in the order in which they are
made ready in the series Texts from Excavations. Reports on
the excavations and catalogues of special categories of objects,
which will include discussions of the inscribed material in its
archaeological context, will be published in the Excavation
Memoirs of the Egypt Exploration Society.

TEXTS FROM EXCAVATIONS

EDITED BY T. G. H. JAMES

FIFTH MEMOIR

CARIAN INSCRIPTIONS FROM NORTH SAQQÂRA AND BUHEN

BY

OLIVIER MASSON

WITH CONTRIBUTIONS BY
GEOFFREY THORNDIKE MARTIN
AND
RICHARD VAUGHAN NICHOLLS

EGYPT EXPLORATION SOCIETY
3 DOUGHTY MEWS, LONDON WCIN 2PG
1978

LONDON

SOLD AT

THE OFFICES OF THE EGYPT EXPLORATION SOCIETY

3 Doughty Mews, London WC1N 2PG

ISSN 0307-5125
ISBN 0 85698 075 7

*Printed in Great Britain
at the University Press, Oxford
by Eric Buckley
Printer to the University*

FOREWORD

In December 1966 the late Professor W. B. Emery, while directing excavations for the Egypt Exploration Society at North Saqqâra, noticed after heavy rain the silhouette of large brick enclosure walls on the eastern scarp of the desert valley which leads westwards from the modern village of Abûsîr southwards towards the Serapeum. These were shown in later seasons to be the enclosure walls of a large temple precinct of the Late Period built on a high terrace. The three sanctuaries situated upon it subsequently proved to be connected with catacombs cut in the rock face. These served respectively for the burial of the Mothers of Apis, of the Baboons, and of the Falcons. It was on 8 December 1968 that the Baboon Catacomb was first entered, and in the preliminary exploration on that day it was immediately observed that in the gallery which branches to the south from the main Upper Baboon Gallery there were scattered on the floor limestone false door stelae inscribed in the Carian script. On the same day, in the floor of the central sanctuary on the temple terrace, there was discovered a rectangular pit lined with reused stelae, containing a deposit of three miniature wooden temple shrines filled with bronze figures of deities and five inlaid wooden statues of Osiris. When the eleven stelae were lifted and examined next day, four proved to bear Egyptianizing votive scenes combined with apparent funerary scenes of alien character and Carian incised inscriptions, while a fifth showed a fine scene of two standing figures which was clearly foreign to Egypt in its technique of execution, and bore a Carian incised inscription. One stela was found to be blank, save for compass-drawn circles in the lunette. These stelae were subsequently recorded and copied in facsimile by G. T. Martin.

The importance of this discovery both for the history of the colony of 'Caromemphite' mercenaries at Memphis and for the decipherment of the Carian script and language was immediately recognized, and was commented upon by Professor Emery in his lecture to the Egypt Exploration Society's Annual General Meeting in 1969. The Society's Committee therefore decided in that year to entrust the scientific publication of the inscriptions on the stelae to one of the world's most distinguished authorities on the Carian script and language, Professor Olivier Masson of the University of Paris (Nanterre) who, to the Society's delight, accepted the commission despite other heavy scholarly commitments. During subsequent seasons at North Saqqâra further fragments of stelae bearing Carian inscriptions were found in various parts of the temple precinct and its southern dependencies, and the records sent to Professor Masson. At a certain stage in his work he asked for a more complete account of the Egyptianizing scenes and Egyptian hieroglyphic inscriptions which appeared on some stelae than I had originally been able to give him. The Society, therefore, asked Dr. G. T. Martin to prepare the section included in this volume. The Society's share of the stelae from the Egyptian Government Antiquities Service's division of antiquities from North Saqqâra in 1969 had meanwhile been divided between various museums contributing to the Society's work. The finest of the stelae with scenes (no. 3) was allocated to the Fitzwilliam Museum at Cambridge, and Mr. R. V. Nicholls, the Keeper of the Department of Antiquities in that museum, took such an interest in them that, as a result of correspondence with Professor Masson, he undertook the task of analysing the Carian scenes and dating them. Thus there came about the fruitful scientific collaboration which has produced this complete publication of the Carian material from North Saqqâra. The Society's deepest gratitude is due to all three scholars.

As over-all responsibility for the publication of the Sacred Animal Necropolis site was conferred upon me by the Society after Professor Emery's death in Cairo in March 1971, it devolves upon me to comment upon the archaeological context of the Carian stelae found there. The final archaeological report on the temple precinct is in preparation, and for technical reasons it is not practicable to publish plans or anticipate conclusions here, but the present state of our understanding may be summarized.

None of the Carian stelae from the site was found in any position for which it could originally have been intended. All of them had either been reused or had been dumped ready for reuse. In the first category come the stelae found lining the deposit in the central sanctuary (nos. **3, 5, 5a, 6, 9, 10**), a block used in the structure of the limestone masonry in the Baboon Gallery (no. **42**) and a fragment reused in the paving of the north–south Sacred Way across the temple precinct (no. **49**). In the second category belong stelae found on the floor of the Baboon Catacomb (nos. **1, 7, 11–33, 39, 41, 44, 47**); it is evident that these had been used, because of their size and thickness, in the ashlar lining of the walls, and the blocking of the baboon niches. Some could have been used for lining the walls of the galleries themselves. Indeed, while every care has been taken to try to identify extant Carian stelae, it is not improbable that if the whole of the masonry linings could be stripped from the interior of the Baboon Catacomb a few more might be found used face-to-the-wall. Another group of Carian stelae was found in one of the rough stone workmen's houses which underlay the fill of the terrace forming the floor of the temple precinct in its final building phase (nos. **34–8, 43, 45a, 46**). Here the stelae were resting against the walls of a house in no meaningful relation to its structure; they had evidently simply been stored by the builders in readiness for reuse in pavements or in lining temple walls.

It is therefore clear that the stelae had been brought from some other site as building material, and that that site must have been systematically looted of stelae. It is inherently probable that the site was near at hand, and that the stelae were easily accessible to the masons of the temple precinct. Since it is overwhelmingly probable that the stelae were funerary in character, and since the temple precinct was situated in the necropolis of Memphis, it is likely that the stelae were taken from the cemetery of the 'Caromemphite' colony. Careful search has been made for this cemetery in the environs of the site without its being identified. If, however, the Carians in Egypt were buried in rock-cut tombs (for or against which supposition there is at present no positive evidence), it is always possible that these tombs were situated in one of the rock faces buried below the buildings of the temple precinct and its southern and western dependencies. Such rock-cut tombs would certainly have been completely cleared during the preliminaries to the construction of the temple buildings. South of the temple enclosure in the lower face of the escarpment there is an unfinished tomb (Vault P) which should belong to the Late Period yet must antedate the building of the Sacred Way outside the South Gate of the temple enclosure. It must, therefore, have been roughly contemporary with the Carian cemetery which could have occupied a similar location; but this is a purely hypothetical suggestion. Wherever the Carian cemetery may be, however, it is doubtful whether extensive and expensive explorations, still less the removal of standing temple buildings, would be adequately rewarded by its discovery, since it would certainly prove to be very completely ruined and looted.

The best evidence for the date and the duration in use of the Carian stelae is that derived from Mr. Nicholls's stylistic analysis of the scenes. All that the evidence from the Sacred Animal Necropolis site can be expected to do is to delimit the date at which the Carian cemetery was looted. The complex architectural history of the temple precinct cannot be set out here. But the following inferences are justified or at the least probable:

i. The stelae found in the workmen's house south of the Baboon Causeway must have been placed there before the filling of the temple platform in this area. This filling must in practice have been contemporary or nearly contemporary with the construction of the north–south Sacred Way across the temple site. This in turn must have been contemporary with the introduction of the South Gate into the main enclosure wall and the completion of the court-yard of the central temple which was decorated and inscribed by Nectanebo II.

ii. The same argument applies to a fragment found in the surface paving of this same Sacred Way.

iii. The stelae lining the pit containing the deposit in the floor of the central sanctuary must, of course, have been placed in position when the deposit was made. The character of the wooden and bronze figures found in the deposit, and the fact that this particular deposit seems by its position to be in the nature of a dedicatory deposit, suggest, though they certainly do not prove, that it was made not later than the time of Nectanebo II.

iv. The Baboon Gate and Chapel were introduced into the main enclosure wall of the temple precinct after its completion. The enclosure wall itself postdates the cutting of the entrance to the Mother of Apis Catacomb, which is likely to have taken place about the time of the earliest Mother of Apis stela found within the Catacomb (Year 1 of Hakoris, 391 B.C.). If the Baboon Catacomb was not begun substantially earlier than the building of the Baboon Gate and Chapel, then the earliest date at which the Carian stelae might have been deposited in the Baboon Catacomb would have been about 380 B.C. In fact, it is likely to have been rather later, as the main group was found in the southern branch of the Upper Gallery, which in the nature of things would not have been excavated until after the main Upper Gallery had been completed and filled with burials.

If these inferences be correct, the probable terminal dates for the reuse of the Carian stelae in building works in the temple precinct are 380–343 B.C. This date in turn provides a terminus for the destruction and looting of the Carian necropolis though these events may, of course, have occurred some years before. The balance of probability may perhaps favour a date early in the fourth century B.C. It is then tempting to speculate whether a burst of nationalist feeling encouraged by the end of Achaemenid Persian rule in 404 B.C. may not have provoked deliberate vengeance on the necropolis of the Carians if, as seems probable, these mercenaries had served the Persian rulers. All, however, that can be said with absolute assurance is that the Carian cemetery must have been pillaged before the end of the reign of Nectanebo II.

For the convenience of scholars, Professor Masson has added to his edition of the Carian stelae from Saqqâra a publication of the Carian inscriptions found or seen by the Society at Buhen in the Sudan during the period 1957–64 (nos. **50–5**).[1] This work was also directed by Professor W. B. Emery, and was a British contribution to the UNESCO campaign to salvage the monuments of Nubia. These inscriptions originally formed part of the structure of the South Temple, decorated by Hatshepsut and Tuthmosis III. They were incised, presumably by Carian mercenaries, on the masonry of the temple, like similar inscriptions on other Nubian temples, when the blocks were *in*

---

[1] The few Greek inscriptions found during the same campaign at Buhen have been published by M. Masson in *Chron. d'Ég.* 51 (1976), 310 ff.

situ, most probably at the time of the Nubian expedition of Psammetichos II.[1] The blocks were either recorded by Sayce and others *in situ* or recovered during the removal of the temple to Khartoum during season 1962–3 and the excavation of the temple in 1963–4.[2] Professor Masson's edition of the inscriptions upon them completes the publication of the inscriptions of Buhen fortress. The Society is deeply grateful to him for undertaking this combined edition of the Carian inscriptions of Saqqâra and Buhen.

H. S. SMITH

[1] S. Sauneron and J. Yoyotte, in *BIFAO* 50 (1952), 157–207.
[2] R. A. Caminos, *The New-Kingdom Temples of Buhen*, i.

53 ff., 57, 71; H. S. Smith *et al.*, *The Fortress of Buhen*, ii. *The Inscriptions* (London, 1976), p. 131.

CONTENTS

LIST OF FIGURES

LIST OF PLATES

PART I

LES INSCRIPTIONS CARIENNES

PAR

OLIVIER MASSON

Professeur à l'Université de Paris X — Nanterre
Directeur d'Études, École pratique des Hautes-
Études — Quatrième Section

AVANT-PROPOS

Il y a déjà quelques années que la tâche de publication des inscriptions cariennes découvertes à Saqqâra-Nord et à Bouhen m'a été confiée par l'Egypt Exploration Society. J'aurais souhaité pouvoir aboutir plus rapidement, mais des occupations diverses m'ont retardé pour la mise en œuvre définitive; en outre, des tâtonnements provoqués par le fait que l'écriture carienne n'est pas complètement déchiffrée ont causé un retard supplémentaire. Maintenant que je peux mettre un point final à la publication, en espérant qu'elle ne sera pas trop imparfaite, il me reste à remercier tous ceux qui ont joué un rôle bénéfique dans la préparation de ce livre: M. H. S. Smith, qui en a suivi toutes les étapes avec compréhension; M. Geoffrey T. Martin, qui avait été chargé de la partie égyptologique du travail et a rédigé une partie du commentaire de ce point de vue; M. Richard V. Nicholls, qui a accepté de s'occuper de l'étude archéologique des stèles à représentation non égyptienne et qui s'est pris d'un grand intérêt pour ces maîtres locaux, des artistes caromemphites; ma femme, qui s'est chargée des nombreux dessins normalisés et des tableaux, les autres dessins ayant été réalisés en Grande-Bretagne, la plupart par M. G. Denning; mon ami Jean Yoyotte, qui suit depuis longtemps mes recherches cariennes; M. Michael Meier (Meier-Brügger), qui s'intéresse depuis 1975 au même domaine et avec qui j'ai discuté plusieurs problèmes; enfin M. T. G. H. James, éditeur des collections de l'Egypt Exploration Society, responsable pour l'impression du volume.

OLIVIER MASSON

Paris, octobre 1976

INTRODUCTION

§ 1. Le présent volume contient essentiellement la publication des stèles, objets divers et fragments portant des inscriptions cariennes (**1** à **49**), qui ont été découverts entre 1968 et 1975 dans les souterrains de Saqqâra-Nord, durant les fouilles de l'Egypt Exploration Society, dirigées d'abord par le regretté W. B. Emery,[1] continuées par MM. G. T. Martin et H. S. Smith. Plusieurs stèles (**1** à **7**), ornées de représentations égyptiennes, égyptisantes ou hellénisantes, et comportant parfois un texte égyptien hiéroglyphique, sont étudiées en détail et à part, deuxième partie, par les soins de MM. G. T. Martin et R. V. Nicholls, aux points de vue de l'épigraphie égyptienne et de l'archéologie.[2]

A ce matériel entièrement inédit, on a ajouté la petite série des inscriptions cariennes de Bouhen (**50** à **55**). Un seul de ces documents (**50**) est inédit, et a été découvert en 1962–1963 par l'expédition de l'Egypt Exploration Society, alors dirigée aussi par W. B. Emery.[3] Mais les autres graffites (à l'exception de **53** et **54**, non retrouvés) ont été revus et copiés à l'occasion des travaux de cette époque, si bien qu'il a semblé opportun de donner ici l'ensemble des graffites cariens de Bouhen.

I. Le matériel

§ 2, 1. Le support matériel des inscriptions des deux sites est de nature très différente. A Bouhen, on a uniquement affaire à des graffites, plus ou moins longs, incisés sur les parois ou les pierres du temple d'Hatshepsout, et laissés par des visiteurs qui étaient probablement des mercenaires.

2. A Saqqâra, en revanche, il doit s'agir à peu près uniquement de stèles funéraires, avec des inscriptions incisées.[4] Sur une cinquantaine de pièces, on peut dénombrer:

(a) Six grandes stèles cintrées, décorées de motifs égyptiens ou égyptisants, ou d'un style grec provincial, **1** à **6** (hauteur 42 à 90 cm.). Elles portent tantôt un texte double, hiéroglyphique et carien, tantôt un texte carien seulement. L'étude complémentaire en est donnée, dans la seconde partie, par G. T. Martin pour **1**, **2**, **4**, **5**, **5a** (anépigraphe), **6**, et par R. V. Nicholls pour **3**, **4**, **5**, **5a**.

(b) Cinq stèles de type rectangulaire ou cintré, mais sans décoration, **7** à **11** (hauteur 30 à 43 cm.). Seule la stèle **7** a reçu un texte double, carien et hiéroglyphique, ce dernier étant étudié par G. T. Martin, seconde partie, **7**. Les autres ont seulement une inscription carienne. A ce groupe, on peut ajouter les fragments **43** (stèle cintrée), peut-être **41** et **42**.

(c) Vingt-sept stèles entières ou presque intactes, du type dit 'fausse-porte', **12** à **38** (hauteur 26 à 42 cm.). Elles ne portent que des inscriptions cariennes.[5]

(d) Objets divers et fragments. Les pièces les plus notables sont: une plaque de calcaire travaillée (26 × 48 cm.), décorée sur la surface, avec inscription incisée sur une des faces latérales, **39**;

---

[1] Informations préliminaires chez W. B. Emery, *JEA* 56 (1970), p. 5–8, avec reproduction de quelques stèles, pl. X, 1–2 et XV, 1–5. Généralités chez H. S. Smith, *A Visit to Ancient Egypt, Life at Memphis and Saqqara* ..., Warminster, 1974, Part II, 'The Sacred Animal Necropolis at North Saqqara'.

[2] On a ajouté à cette série une stèle provenant d'Abousîr, dont l'inscription est à considérer comme carienne, et non pas grecque; voir Part II, pp. 64, 91, commentaire de **3**, etc., et Appendice I.

[3] Voir W. B. Emery, *Kush* 12 (1964), p. 43–46 (sans mention du graffite carien).

[4] Dans le cas particulier de **13a**, on a affaire à une inscription peinte, qui s'est presque complètement effacée.

[5] Il existe aussi une stèle fausse-porte anépigraphe, H5–1843 (British Museum 67237); elle n'a jamais été utilisée, à moins qu'un texte peint n'ait complètement disparu (voir note précédente).

la destination de cette plaque ne m'est pas connue. D'autres plaques ou blocs de calcaire incisés de manières diverses, **40** à **42**, pourraient représenter des stèles plus ou moins grossières.[1] En outre, des fragments divers, qui appartiennent le plus souvent à des stèles 'fausse-porte', **44**, etc.

3. L'énumération de ces divers 'supports' ne laisse aucun doute sur le caractère ouvertement funéraire de ces objets, à l'exception éventuellement de la plaque décorée, **39**.[2] Les trois types de stèles retrouvés à Saqqâra, avec une majorité remarquable pour le type 'fausse-porte', correspondent d'ailleurs à des types connus du matériel funéraire égyptien, ce caractère étant souligné dans les textes hiéroglyphiques de quelques pièces.

4. Il n'est donc pas étonnant que cette répartition entre trois types principaux vienne nous rappeler exactement la composition du matériel qui était disponible avant les fouilles de Saqqâra-Nord. Parmi les pièces qui avaient été rassemblées en 1956,[3] ce n'est probablement pas un hasard si nous trouvons précisément: (*a*) quatre stèles à décor égyptien, **44, 46, 43, 48** bis F = **E** à **H** M–Y, provenant de 'Memphis' ou de Saqqâra; (*b*) deux stèles cintrées, **74** et **48** F = **C** et **D** M–Y, la première sans provenance, la seconde de 'Memphis'; (*c*) seulement deux stèles 'fausse-porte', **47** et **47** bis F = **A** et **B** M–Y, encore de 'Memphis'. Il est donc très probable que ces stèles, dont la plupart n'ont pas été mises au jour par des fouilles officielles, et sont souvent attribuées d'une manière vague à 'Memphis', doivent provenir, en dernière analyse, de la même nécropole carienne qui a enrichi les fouilles de Saqqâra-Nord, sinon des mêmes souterrains.

§ 3. En l'absence de toute donnée positive qui serait fournie par un déchiffrement des textes eux-mêmes, où nous trouverions probablement des indications sur l'origine des défunts,[4] nous pouvons tout de même conclure sans grand risque d'erreur qu'il a existé dans la périphérie de Memphis,[5] en relation avec le quartier carien ou *Karikon* de certaines sources grecques,[6] un ou plusieurs cimetières de Cariens.[7] C'est dans ces nécropoles, désaffectées à une date inconnue, que les Égyptiens qui ont aménagé les souterrains de Saqqâra-Nord ont dû prendre les stèles, afin de les remployer pour boucher des niches ou à d'autres fins.[8] Selon toute vraisemblance, ces Cariens de Memphis étaient de même origine que ceux que nous voyons appelés à un certain moment *Karomemphitai* ou 'Caromemphites' et qui sont encore mentionnés dans des documents du IIIe siècle avant notre ère.[9]

§ 4. Pour la chronologie des stèles de Saqqâra, seules les stèles décorées du groupe A peuvent nous apporter des renseignements assez précis. Les analyses précises de leur typologie par G. T. Martin et R. V. Nicholls permettent de les placer, en chiffres ronds, entre 550 et 500 avant notre ère.[10] Cette datation correspond à celle qui a été proposée en 1956 pour les stèles datables qui

[1] La gravure de **40** est d'un type spécial: les lettres ont commencé à être tracées en pointillé, mais le travail n'a pas été achevé.

[2] Il pourrait s'agir d'une plaque prévue pour un usage non funéraire, remployée par le graveur carien en guise de stèle.

[3] Pour les références abrégées, où D = Deroy, F = Friedrich, M–Y = Masson–Yoyotte, Š = Ševoroškin, voir les Abréviations bibliographiques, p. 19; de même pour la brochure de Zauzich, *Inschriften*.

[4] On ne tient pas compte ici du pseudo-déchiffrement de Zauzich, *Inschriften*, qui a cru retrouver dans certains de nos textes des personnages originaires de diverses contrées.

[5] Au nord de la ville, selon J. Yoyotte, *BIFAO* 71 (1972), p. 10.

[6] En dernier lieu, O. Masson, 'Le nom des Cariens dans quelques langues de l'antiquité', *Mélanges linguistiques offerts à E. Benveniste*, Paris, 1975, p. 408.

[7] Ajouter également la région d'Abousîr, avec la stèle republiée ici, Appendice I, etc.

[8] Voir déjà W. B. Emery, *JEA* 56 (1970), p. 6: 'the stelae . . . must be earlier than the fourth century B.C. and were perhaps removed from a Carian burial ground in an adjacent area when Nectanebo built his small temple'; de même G. T. Martin, *JEA* 59 (1973), p. 10; H. S. Smith, *A Visit to Ancient Egypt*, p. 43.

[9] O. Masson, article cité, p. 408; aussi, p. 412–413, pour l'identification (avec J. Yoyotte) de *Grmnfi* comme nom hiéroglyphique de ces Caromemphites, au temple de Kom Ombo.

[10] Voir leur commentaire, Part II.

étaient connues avant les fouilles de Saqqâra-Nord: après 568, c'est-à-dire après l'installation à Memphis des mercenaires cariens auparavant stationnés dans le Delta oriental, sous Amasis, et probablement au début du règne de ce pharaon.[1] Il n'y a pas d'objection, semble-t-il, pour placer dans la seconde moitié du VIe siècle l'ensemble de la documentation de Saqqâra-Nord. Dans ces conditions, il est évident que cette série est plus récente que les graffites cariens d'Abou-Simbel, qui doivent être l'œuvre, vers 591, de mercenaires cariens alors incorporés aux troupes étrangères de Psammétique II, lors de sa campagne nubienne.[2] Par extrapolation, on a le droit de proposer une date analogue pour les graffites cariens de Bouhen, cette avancée extrême des Cariens vers le sud ne pouvant se comprendre qu'en relation avec la campagne nubienne de Psammétique II.[3]

§ 5, 1. Sur les Caromemphites du VIe siècle avant notre ère, quels sont les renseignements que nous apporte cette documentation? Faute de pouvoir lire véritablement les textes, nous devons nous contenter d'interroger les représentations figurées. Heureusement, quelques-unes des stèles sont d'un intérêt exceptionnel à ce point de vue. La plus précieuse, 3, décorée avec le motif d'une jeune femme et d'un jeune homme se saluant, dans un beau style gréco-oriental, nous montre à l'évidence deux Cariens de Memphis. Le caractère de ce document est unique, comme le montre R. V. Nicholls dans son commentaire très érudit; l'iconographie de la Carie elle-même ne nous a rien fourni jusqu'ici de comparable, et nous voyons ici un rare témoignage du développement d'un art carien à Memphis, mêlant à une origine gréco-asiatique des influences proprement égyptiennes. Une autre belle stèle, 4, porte dans son registre inférieur une scène funéraire qui n'est pas égyptienne, la *prothesis* ou exposition d'une défunte, sur un lit funéraire, avec la présence de plusieurs personnages. Dans un style plus sommaire, les stèles 5 et 5a représentent, au même emplacement, la *prothesis* d'un défunt et d'une défunte. Dans tous ces cas, il s'agit évidemment de Cariens d'Égypte.[4]

2. Les stèles non décorées de la série B ne nous apportent rien de comparable. Plus remarquables sont peut-être les stèles 'fausse-porte', qui constituent la majeure partie du matériel. A propos des deux seules stèles de ce type connues avant 1956, on avait souligné le caractère égyptien de ces stèles, en indiquant cependant que leur emploi n'était pas courant dans l'Égypte pharaonique, sous les XXVIe et XXVIIe dynasties.[5] Le grand nombre de stèles découvertes à Saqqâra-Nord montre que ce type de monument funéraire a été particulièrement affectionné par les Cariens de Memphis, pour des raisons que nous ignorons. Il n'est peut-être pas trop hardi de supposer que ces stèles auraient rappelé, en quelque sorte en miniature, certaines tombes rupestres à 'fausse-porte', lesquelles sont connues en Asie Mineure, particulièrement en Lycie, et qui ont pu exister en Carie même.[6]

[1] Masson–Yoyotte, *Objets*, p. 2 (lire naturellement 568 *avant* notre ère), et tableau après la p. 72.

[2] O. Masson, 'Les Cariens en Égypte', *Bull. Société Française d'Égyptologie* 56, novembre 1969, p. 30–31.

[3] Encore plus loin, au sud-ouest de Bouhen, se situe le témoignage le plus méridional laissé par des Cariens, le graffite solitaire du Gebel Sheik Suleiman, 72 F = 85 Š.

[4] Des comparaisons intéressantes peuvent être faites avec des stèles araméennes, qui proviennent souvent de Saqqâra; voir plus loin les remarques de R. V. Nicholls, Part II, pp. 66–67, à propos de 3. En particulier, sur une stèle de Bruxelles, récemment republiée par E. Lipiński, *Chronique d'Égypte*, 50 (1975), p. 93–104, le corps de la défunte est représenté, sans vêtements.

[5] Masson–Yoyotte, *Objets*, p. 1 n. 1, où il est rappelé que

l'on connaît seulement deux stèles du type 'fausse-porte' avec inscription funéraire en grec. La première, *Sammelbuch* 4300, provient précisément de Saqqâra; réédition par K. Herbert, *Greek and Latin Inscriptions in the Brooklyn Museum*, Brooklyn, 1972, p. 11–12, no. 1, pl. I (datation vers 570–520). La seconde, *Sammelbuch* 4537, vient de Naukratis; réédition par A. Bernand, *Le Delta égyptien*, 1. *Les confins libyques*, Le Caire, 1970, p. 761–762, no. 31, pl. 40, 4 (datation encore incertaine; assurément plus récente que l'autre).

[6] Malheureusement, l'architecture funéraire de la Carie archaïque n'est pas connue; comme a bien voulu me le préciser M. P. Roos, les tombes rupestres à façade ne sont pas antérieures au IVe s., dans l'état actuel de la documentation. En Lycie, en tout cas, le motif architectural de la 'fausse-porte' est utilisé pour des tombes rupestres: par exemple P.

II. L'alphabet et les problèmes de transcription

§ 6, 1. Avant d'examiner la structure des inscriptions, il convient d'étudier, dans la mesure de nos moyens, l'écriture qui est utilisée dans nos documents de Saqqâra et de Bouhen. Pour la commodité, mais aussi en accord avec les plus récentes recherches dans ce domaine, nous parlerons désormais d'un 'alphabet',[1] en écartant la vieille hypothèse qui faisait intervenir des signes à valeur syllabique (§ 7, 1).

2. L'alphabet qui apparaît à Saqqâra et à Bouhen représente, en gros, celui qui était déjà connu pour le carien d'Égypte, soit environ trente-trois lettres.[2] Ne sont pas utilisés les signes *8*,[3] *13*[4] et *37*;[5] le signe *40*, en forme de flèche, est présent sur les deux sites.

3. En revanche, on trouve apparemment trois signes nouveaux:

42 6; en forme de 6, ce signe n'est attesté qu'à Saqqâra, dans **26** (deux exemples), **33** (deux exemples). Il est possible qu'il s'agisse d'une variante d'un autre signe, mais je ne peux présenter aucune hypothèse dans ce sens. Une interprétation comme *b*, fondée sur une certaine ressemblance extérieure, a été proposée par Zauzich: elle n'a rien de convaincant.[6]

43 𝑦; d'une forme difficile à décrire, ce signe se trouve, en tout cas, employé à Saqqâra comme à Bouhen. Pour Saqqâra, **9**, début du dernier mot; **39**, au milieu du second mot; à Bouhen, **50**, ligne 4 (même graphie), et (sous toute réserve), **51**, ligne 5, même mot, mais signe très détérioré. Je n'ai pas d'interprétation à proposer pour ce signe.

44 𝔶; autre forme notable. C'est un *hapax* à Saqqâra, **29**, dernier mot. On pourrait se demander s'il ne s'agit pas de *43*, renversé? Un rapprochement avec d'autres signes n'est pas plausible.[7]

§ 7, 1. On sait quelle incertitude règne toujours pour la transcription du carien, aucun des systèmes qui ont été proposés depuis la fin du XIXᵉ s. n'ayant abouti à un déchiffrement incontesté. J'ai hésité moi-même, depuis le début de mes recherches, entre différents procédés, tels que: maintien, à titre de convention, de la transcription mi-alphabétique, mi-syllabique de Bork et Friedrich,[8] au besoin en soulignant son aspect conventionnel par l'insertion de guillemets;[9] adoption intégrale de la transcription proposée depuis 1964 par V. Ševoroškin,[10] ou bien introduction de quelques modifications à ce système, avec R. Gusmani;[11] emploi d'un mélange de transcriptions latines pour les lettres banales et de dessins pour les signes difficiles ou rares, ainsi ⊕ = *25*, □ = *27*, etc., comme l'a fait à l'occasion P. Meriggi,[12] procédé qui aurait certainement des inconvénients pour la typographie s'il était généralisé; utilisation d'une transcription entièrement chiffrée, *1* pour A, etc., ce qui rendrait les comparaisons difficiles et les index délicats à manier. D'autre part, il aurait été particulièrement inopportun d'introduire ici l'une ou l'autre des

---

Demargne, *Fouilles de Xanthos*, i (1958), p. 116–125; v (1974), p. 34–35. Dans d'autres régions de l'Asie Mineure, on trouve à date tardive des stèles avec des 'fausses-portes': ainsi en Phrygie, bibliographie chez J. et L. Robert, *Rev. Ét. Gr.* 85 (1972), *Bull. Épigr.* no. 458; aussi en Bithynie, G. Mendel, *BCH* 33 (1909), p. 321–327.

[1] O. Masson, *BSL* 68 (1973), p. 190–191.

[2] Les chiffres correspondant aux lettres cariennes sont ceux du tableau général, fig. 1, ou du tableau paléographique, figs. 2–3.

[3] Il apparaît en Égypte sur un bronze, 45 F = *K* M–Y.

[4] Il se rencontre à Abou-Simbel et à Silsile, § 8.

[5] Pour ce signe, voir *Kadmos* 15 (1976), p. 83.

[6] Zauzich, *Inschriften*, p. 19; en dernier lieu, Th. Kowalski, *Kadmos* 14 (1975), tableau de la p. 74, rapproche notre signe

25, soit pour lui *ļ*.

[7] Zauzich, op. cit., p. 22, a supposé une variante de notre signe *29*, ce qui ne paraît nullement convaincant; selon Kowalski, loc. cit., ce serait une dentale (no. 25, formes très diverses).

[8] Ainsi chez Masson–Yoyotte, *Objets*, 1956 (cf. p. xii, n. 1).

[9] *Kratylos* 18 (1973), p. 40; *Kadmos* 13 (1974), p. 124 sqq.

[10] Premier état dans *RHA* xxii (1964), p. 1–55; *Issledovanija*, 1965; un tableau un peu modifié a été mis en circulation en 1975.

[11] *Neue epichorische Schriftzeugnisse aus Sardis (1958–1971)*, Cambridge, Mass., 1975, chapitre 3, p. 81–105.

[12] *Kadmos* 5 (1966), p. 85 sqq.; *Europa, Festschrift Grumach*, 1967, p. 218–228.

transcriptions 'révolutionnaires' qui ont été proposées en ces dernières années, et qui n'ont pas apporté de progrès.[1]

2. Dans ces conditions — et faute de mieux — je me suis résolu à adopter un procédé mixte qui est déjà employé pour certaines écritures non entièrement déchiffrées, à savoir un mélange de transcriptions latines simples (évitant l'emploi de majuscules, et surtout, de lettres grecques)[2] et de chiffres, ces derniers correspondant au numéro d'ordre du signe dans le tableau général à trois colonnes (fig. 1).[3] Ce procédé, comme les autres, n'est pas dépourvu d'inconvénients. La disposition générale, avec les lettres d'aspect grec au début, *1* à *23*, et celles d'aspect 'épichorique' ensuite, *24* à *45*, comporte sa part d'arbitraire, et vise seulement à être commode. Ce qui est plus grave, c'est que le choix, pour les transcriptions, entre les lettres latines et les chiffres, ne peut se faire, trop souvent, que selon des critères purement subjectifs; malgré la gêne qui en résulte pour le lecteur, la prudence m'a incité à laisser de nombreuses transcriptions par chiffres, notamment de *27* à *45*. Mais d'autre part, la présence des transcriptions en lettres latines peut faire croire à l'utilisateur pressé qu'il s'agit là de valeurs démontrées, et non pas de lectures plus ou moins théoriques. J'ai essayé de remédier à ce dernier défaut en plaçant un point d'interrogation à la droite d'un certain nombre de lettres, dans le tableau général (mais non pas dans les transcriptions de textes ou de mots): par exemple, si A, O, V/Y semblent bien correspondre à *a*, *o*, *u*, pour C, E, T, nous dirons, sous toute réserve, *g?*, *é?*, *t?*, etc. Le nombre de ces points d'interrogation est éloquent et doit nous rappeler à chaque instant le caractère conventionnel de la transcription. Il est impossible d'évaluer avec précision le degré de plausibilité de chacune de ces transcriptions: on essaiera seulement d'en donner une idée, à propos d'un certain nombre de lettres.

3. Dans le tableau général qui est reproduit ici (fig. 1), on a tenté, sans trop multiplier les variantes, de représenter l'écriture, ou plutôt, les écritures cariennes, par l'utilisation de trois colonnes qui correspondent à trois grandes subdivisions.

COLONNE I: le carien de Carie, à l'exception, pour l'extrême sud, de Kaunos et de sa région (soit les textes 14 à 16 D, plus un fragment nouveau de 16); pour d'autres raisons, on a complètement omis les témoignages assez aberrants de Chalkétor et de Labranda (4 et 17 D).[4] On y rattache l'écriture des rares monnaies à légende carienne[5] et celle de la bilingue trouvée à Athènes en 1954.[6]

COLONNE II: le carien propre à Kaunos et à sa région, tel qu'il vient d'être défini.[7]

COLONNE III: le carien d'Égypte (bronzes et objets divers; stèles; graffites); on a laissé de côté 38 F, l'ostrakon de Hou.[8]

§ 8. Ce tableau fournit l'occasion de donner un certain nombre de remarques sur les lettres cariennes, en insistant sur le répertoire du carien d'Égypte et, naturellement, sur l'apport des

---

[1] Dans les travaux de R. Shafer, I. Otkupščikov, K.-Th. Zauzich, Th. Kowalski; cf. O. Masson, *BSL* 68 (1973), p. 190–198.

[2] Ces dernières, outre la complication typographique, sont d'un emploi peu commode lorsqu'il faut distinguer un *v* (*nu*) grec et un *v* latin, par exemple (transcriptions de Ševoroškin).

[3] Ce tableau, diffusé de manière provisoire depuis juin 1975, a été publié dans *Kadmos* 15 (1976), tableau après la p. 82 (planche III).

[4] Soit les colonnes 4 et 17 dans le tableau de L. Deroy, *Antiquité Classique* 24 (1955), p. 332–333. Pour une inscription analogue de Chalkétor, voir G. Neumann, *Kadmos* 8

[1969], p. 152–157.

[5] Deux ont été republiées par O. Masson, *Kadmos* 13 (1974), p. 124–130.

[6] En dernier lieu, O. Masson, *BSL* 68 (1973), p. 198–205; ajouter à la bibliographie V. Georgiev, *Kadmos* 14 (1975), p. 64–67.

[7] Une étude des inscriptions de Kaunos est donnée par O. Masson dans *Anadolu* (*Anatolia*), 17 (1973), p. 123–131, à l'occasion de la publication du fragment nouveau de 16 D (découvert à Kaunos en 1971, fouilles de B. Öğün).

[8] Réédité par O. Masson, *Europa, Festschrift Grumach*, 1967, p. 211–217, pl. XX.

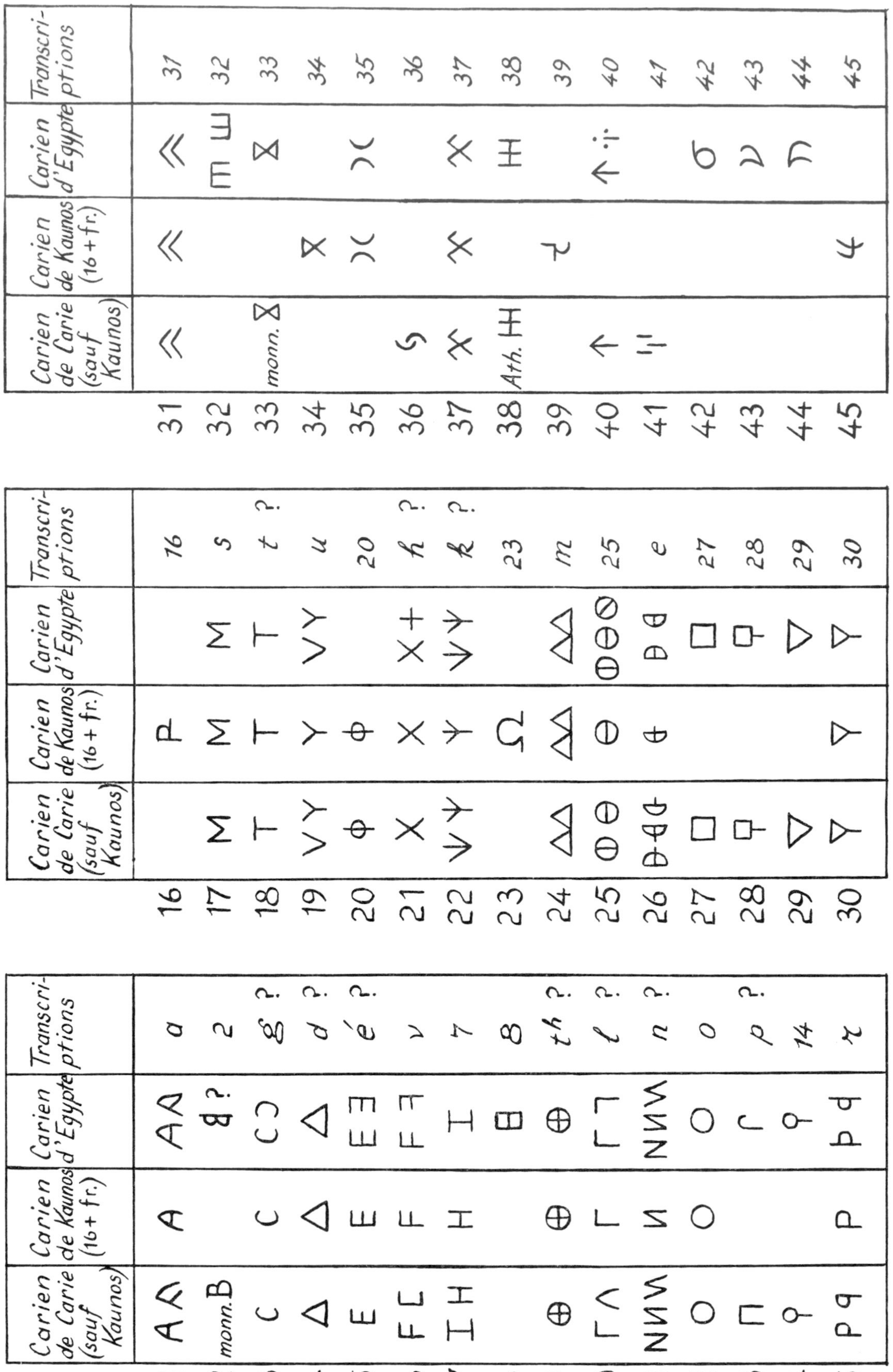

Carien de Carie (sauf Kaunos)	Carien de Kaunos (16+fr.)	Carien d'Egypte	Transcriptions
1			a
2 monn.			2
3			g?
4			d?
5			é?
6			v
7			7
8			8
9			th?
10			l?
11			n?
12			o
13			p?
14			14
15			r

Carien de Carie (sauf Kaunos)	Carien de Kaunos (16+fr.)	Carien d'Egypte	Transcriptions
16			16
17			s
18			t?
19			u
20			20
21			h?
22			ḱ?
23			23
24			m
25			25
26			e
27			27
28			28
29			29
30			30

Carien de Carie (sauf Kaunos)	Carien de Kaunos (16+fr.)	Carien d'Egypte	Transcriptions
31			31
32			32
33 monn.			33
34			34
35			35
36			36
37			37
38 Ath.			38
39			39
40			40
41			41
42			42
43			43
44			44
45			45

FIG. 1. Tableau des transcriptions proposées pour les trois principaux types d'écriture carienne

nouvelles inscriptions.[1] Il est complété ici par un tableau paléographique (fig. 2–3), qui montre les principales variantes utilisées à Saqqâra (col. II) et à Bouhen (col. III).

2. La lettre B apparaît avec certitude sur des monnaies de Carie.[2] En Égypte, elle est pratiquement inconnue, à l'exception d'alphabets aberrants.[3] Il faut renoncer à une lecture *b* sur la stèle 46 F = **F** M–Y, signe 4.[4]

3, 4. Les transcriptions par *g* et *d* sont souvent adoptées, mais elles demeurent conventionnelles.

5. Le signe en forme d'*epsilon* est assez fréquent à Saqqâra: voir **1, 14, 17, 21, 25, 38, 44, 48d**; à Bouhen, **53** (?), **55**. Il montre régulièrement la forme de la lettre grecque archaïque (haste verticale dépassant en bas). Comme on sait, le lydien a ꟼ (sinistroverse) pour *e*, le lycien a E pour *i*; ici aussi, il doit s'agir d'une voyelle. Avec Ševoroškin,[5] je transcris par *é*, ce qui permet de différencier commodément *5* de *26* ou *e* (e bref); la ressemblance entre les deux phonèmes est indiquée par le parallélisme de deux mots de Saqqâra, *a-v-14-a-é-25*, **14**, et *r-a-v-k-a-e-25*, **9**. Ailleurs, *é* est souvent employé à côté de *a* ou *e*; remarquer encore des séquences initiales telles que *é-e-a*, **17**; *é-e-25*, **38**; peut-être *e-é-v* à Bouhen, **53**.

6. En Carie même et à Athènes, Ⅽ qui est connu comme une variante grecque du *digamma*, doit représenter aussi une variante de F et ꟻ; cependant, elle est introuvable en Égypte.[6] La notation par *v* (ou une valeur analogue) demeure séduisante.[7]

7. On admet ici, avec Ševoroškin, l'équivalence de Ɪ et ʜ, mais sans donner de transcription.

8. Pour l'Égypte, on fait figurer à part le signe ⯊ qui est un hapax sur **45** F, et demeure inconnu à Saqqâra comme à Bouhen.[8] Cette lettre n'existe pas en Carie même, mais est apparue en carien de Sardes.[9]

9. Le signe en forme de *théta* est généralement considéré comme une dentale. Pour le différencier clairement de *18* ou T, rare mais bien attesté à Saqqâra, je transcris *th* (c'est-à-dire t^h) en face de *t*.

11. Depuis Sayce, on a longtemps gardé l'habitude de distinguer un signe spécial ꟺ ou *vu*, en face de ꟿ (sinistroverse) ou ɴ (dextroverse), lequel serait *n*. Encore récemment, Ševoroškin transcrivait avec deux valeurs, soit *b* et *n*.[10] Mais une solution radicale a été préconisée par P. Meriggi, à savoir de renoncer à la distinction entre deux signes, et de voir partout des *n*.[11] Je me suis rallié en 1975 à cette opinion, d'où la valeur *n* qui est proposée ici, avec réserve, pour les trois colonnes.[12]

Peu de temps après, toutefois, la discussion a été renouvelée lorsque Michael Meier a proposé, de manière très ingénieuse, de lire à peu près comme *χ-b-a-d-e* la séquence Ⓒꟿꟷⅅℇ qui apparaît deux fois dans la grande inscription de Kaunos, 16 D = 108 Š, lignes 8 et 12:[13] il s'agirait du nom *carien* de Kaunos, qui correspondrait au lycien *χbide*, révélé par la grande inscription

---

[1] Le tableau chez Masson–Yoyotte, *Objets*, p. 67 (fig. 29) est dépassé.

[2] Emission du type 18b D; voir *Kadmos* 16 (1977), p. 87–88.

[3] Ainsi sur l'ostrakon de Hou, 38 F, ou à Silsile, 62 F.

[4] On doit reconnaître un *r*: voir plus loin, commentaire de **50**, ligne 2, et Appendice II.

[5] *Kadmos* 7 (1968), tableau après la p. 172 (antérieurement, transcriptions par ε ou par E majuscule).

[6] O. Masson, *BSL* 68 (1973), p. 203–204.

[7] Cf. *Kadmos* 13 (1974), p. 131–132, à propos de *m-e-s-e-v-e*, 1 F.

[8] Selon des hypothèses de Ševoroškin, *Issledovanija*, p. 315 et 310, cette forme (qu'il transcrit e_1) se trouverait à Silsile,

[9] O. Masson, *Kadmos* 6 (1967), p. 132. Voir maintenant R. Gusmani, *Epichorische Schriftzeugnisse aus Sardis*, p. 90 et 92. Ce dernier, suivant une suggestion de P. Meriggi, transcrit par *à* (donc une variante de *a*).

53 F = 61 Š, 55 F = 63 Š; malheureusement, le texte de ces graffites est mal établi.

[10] *Issledovanija*, p. 178 sqq. et passim; *RHA* 1964, p. 21 et 26, etc.

[11] P. Meriggi, *Kadmos* 5 (1966), p. 87 n. 17.

[12] En premier lieu, *Kadmos* 15 (1976), p. 83, et tableau, planche III; ibid. 16 (1977), p. 89–91.

[13] M. Meier, 'Zum karischen Namen von Kaunos', *Münchener Studien zur Sprachwissenschaft* 34 (1976), p. 95–100.

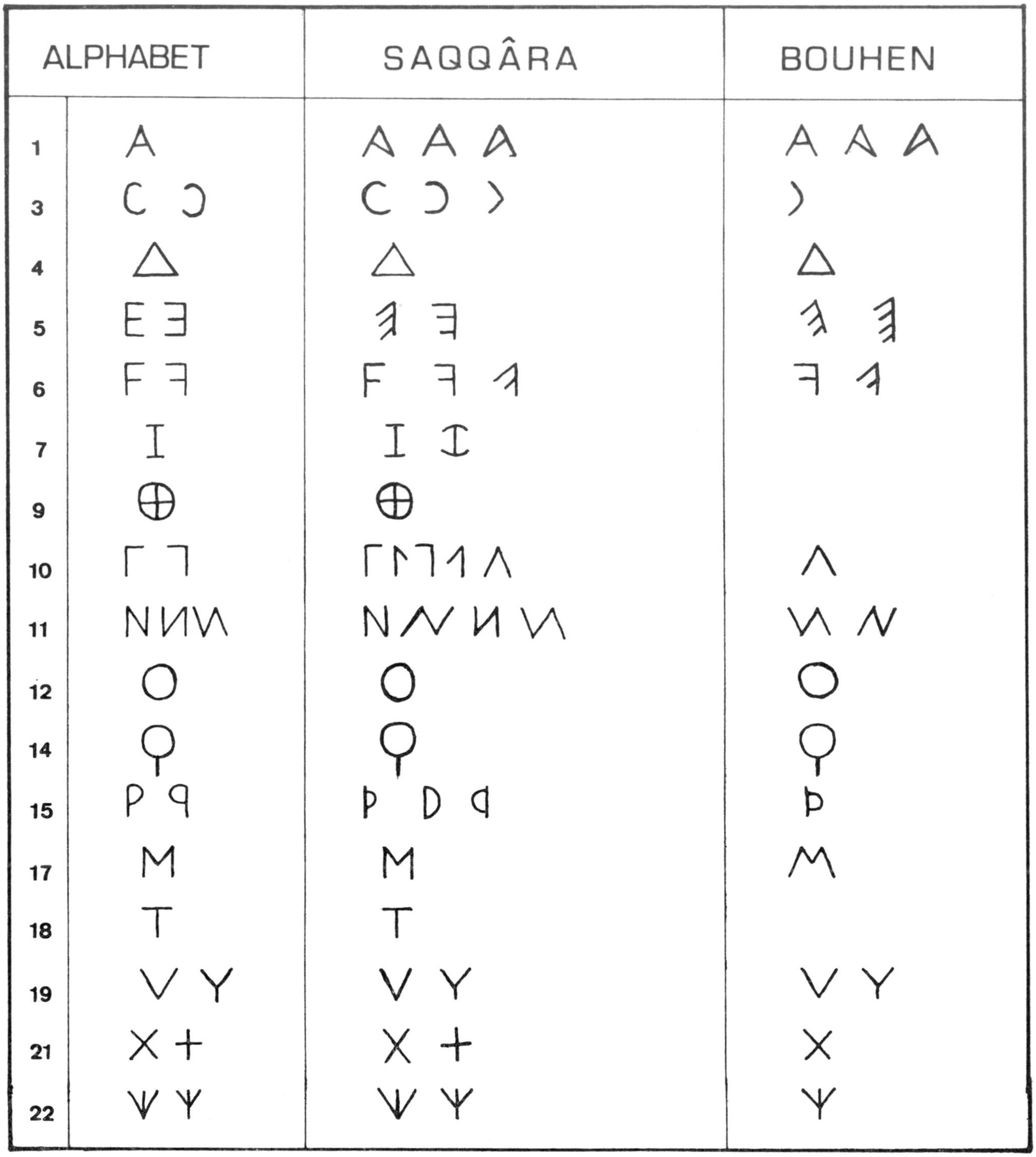

	ALPHABET	SAQQÂRA	BOUHEN
1	Ꭺ	Ꭺ Ꭺ Ꭺ	Ꭺ Ꭺ Ꭺ
3	C ꓚ	C ꓚ ˃	˃
4	△	△	△
5	E ⅎ	ⅎ ⅎ	ⅎ ⅎ
6	F ⅎ	F ⅎ ⅎ	ⅎ ⅎ
7	I ꛁ	I ꛁ	
9	⊕	⊕	
10	Γ ꓶ	Γ ꓶ ⅂ ∧	∧
11	N Ʌ И	N Ʌ И И	И Ʌ
12	O	O	O
14	♀	♀	♀
15	Þ ꟼ	Þ ꟼ ꟼ	Þ
17	M	M	Ɯ
18	T	T	
19	V Y	V Y	V Y
21	X +	X +	X
22	Ѵ Ѱ	Ѵ Ѱ	Ѱ

Fig. 2. Tableau paléographique des signes de Saqqâra et de Bouhen (A)

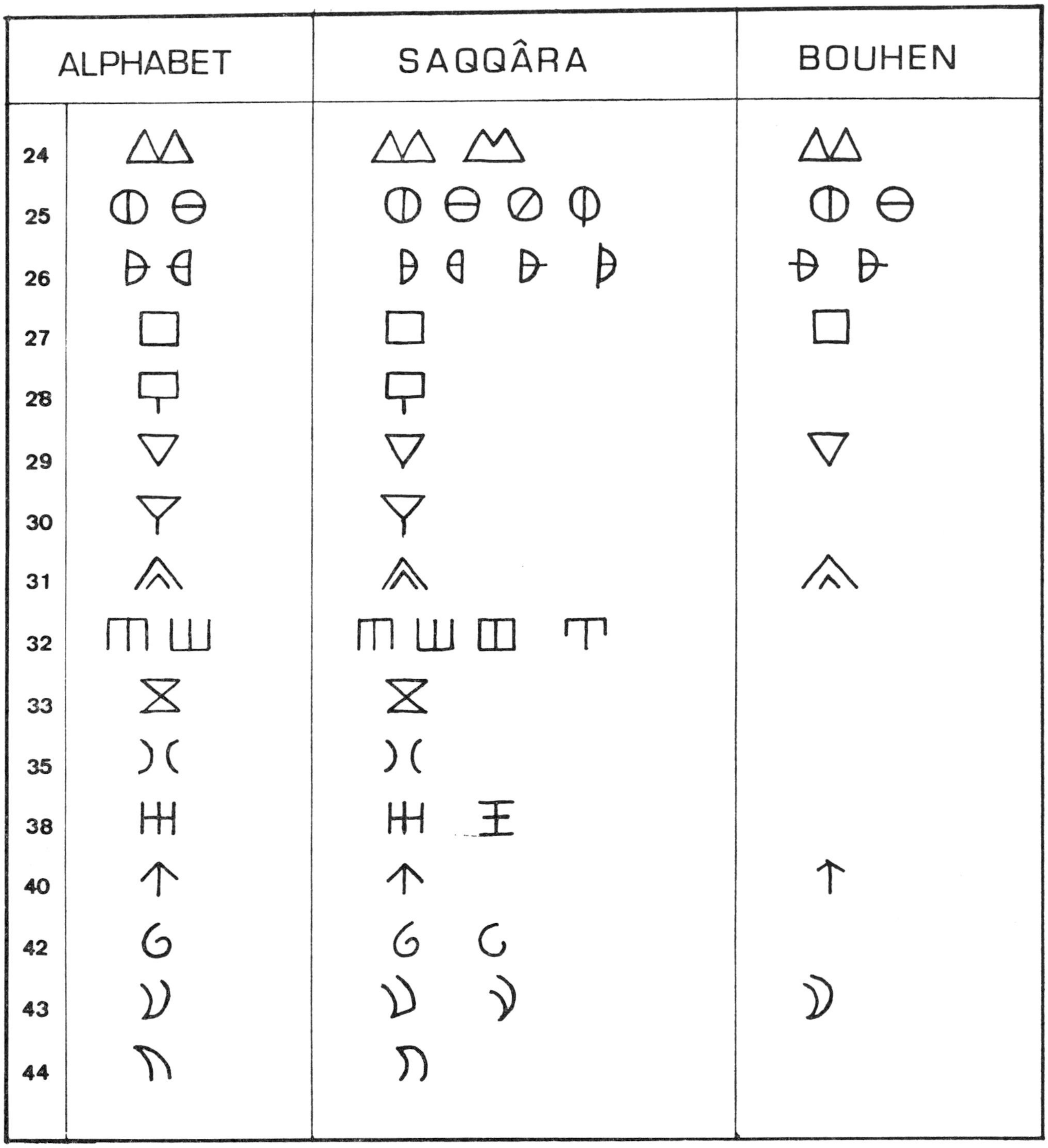

FIG. 3. Tableau paléographique des signes de Saqqâra et de Bouhen (B)

trilingue de Xanthos.[1] Une valeur *b* pourrait donc être acceptée pour le carien de Kaunos, dont le répertoire graphique a, de toute manière, sa physionomie propre.[2] Mais il serait difficile d'adopter la transcription *b* en carien d'Égypte, car les exemples seraient trop nombreux pour un phonème de cette série.

C'est pourquoi, sans chercher à modifier la transcription des textes de Saqqâra et de Bouhen qui avait été rédigée en 1975, j'ai conservé ici la notation provisoire par *n*. Il semble qu'on rencontre le N ordinaire dans les documents rédigés en écriture dextroverse, par exemple **3** à **6**, **15**, **16**, **32**, **37**, et le И ou Ͷ, normalement, en écriture sinistroverse, par exemple **8** à **13**, **24**, **26**, **27**, **31**, **34** à **36**, etc. L'emploi du N dans certains textes sinistroverses serait dû à une confusion bien compréhensible : des exemples sont clairs à Saqqâra, ainsi **17**, **19**, **21**, **23**, **25**. En outre, la présence simultanée de N et de И se rencontre ici, **19**, **20**, **25**;[3] également à Bouhen, **53** et **54**, si les copies sont exactes.[4]

13. Correspondant apparemment au *pi* grec, ce signe demeure rare. Un exemple (à branches égales) dans une épitaphe de Kaunos récemment publiée,[5] mais dont l'alphabet semble différent du 'caunien' proprement dit. En Égypte, c'est seulement à Abou-Simbel et à Silsile qu'on rencontre des exemples de cette lettre, avec une forme carrée, 73 Š, plus souvent arrondie, 78 Š, 39 et 62 F.

14. Le signe fréquent en forme de Ϙ ou *qoppa* grec est placé ici d'un point de vue purement formel, et laissé sans transcription. On y a vu le plus souvent une voyelle : *ä* pour Sayce et Sundwall, *i* pour Ševoroškin.[6] Pour sa part, P. Meriggi reconnaît simplement *q*, soit le *qoppa*.[7] En dernière analyse, il me semble que cette dernière solution est très plausible, et recommandée par certaines formes de Saqqâra : voir **14**, commentaire, ainsi que **36** pour une alternance avec *g*. Toutefois, par prudence, je maintiens ici la transcription en chiffres.[8]

15. La transcription par *r* devrait être correcte, si l'on se fie au témoignage de la monnaie lycienne pourvue des lettres cariennes, *e–r*, 76 F.[9]

17. On y voit généralement le représentant du *san*, c'est-à-dire *s*.[10]

18. Le signe en forme de *tau* est bien attesté à Saqqâra, quoique rarement, voir **19** et **23**. La transcription *t* est conventionnelle, mais on a cette valeur en lycien et en lydien. D'autre part, je doute du rapprochement fait par Ševoroškin[11] avec la flèche, *40*; ces lettres sont bien distinctes à Saqqâra.[12]

20. Le signe de forme *phi* semble propre à la Carie et à Kaunos, et je pense qu'il faut le distinguer de *25* Ⓞ Θ. Cependant, à l'occasion, la haste verticale de *25* peut dépasser en bas, et donner un aspect de *phi* : ainsi à Saqqâra, **30**; surtout à Abou-Simbel, 72, 75 et 77 Š.

21. Les deux formes, X ou +, existent à Saqqâra. La valeur *h* (comme en lycien), conservée par Ševoroškin, demeure conventionnelle.

[1] E. Laroche, *CRAI* 1974, p. 122.

[2] O. Masson, *Anadolu* 17 (1973), p. 127–131.

[3] Dans **25**, texte sinistroverse, on voit quatre exemples de N contre un seul de И.

[4] L'examen des treize exemples fournis par les mots à radical *n-32-g-o* montre aussi l'équivalence des trois formes : N dans les textes dextroverses (**4**, **5**, **6**, **32**) et parfois dans les sinistroverses (**21** et **23**); И ou la forme penchée Ͷ dans les sinistroverses (**8**, **12**, **20**, **24**, **27**, **34**, **38**).

[5] P. Roos (et F. Steinherr), *The Rock-Tombs of Caunus* i, 1972, p. 109.

[6] *RHA* 1964, p. 18, etc. Un peu autrement, *j* chez Gusmani, op. cit., p. 90, 92.

[7] *Europa, Festschrift Grumach*, p. 218, 225.

[8] Pour une discussion détaillée, voir *Kadmos* 16 (1977), p. 91–4.

[9] *Kadmos* 13 (1974), p. 127–130.

[10] Ibid., p. 132.

[11] *RHA* 1964 p. 12–13, etc.; *Klio* 50 (1968), p. 55 sqq.

[12] Vu la rareté du T dans les nouveaux documents, on ne voit rien de nouveau pour les rapports de cette lettre avec le T valant *ss* dans plusieurs alphabets grecs d'Asie Mineure, notamment à Halicarnasse. Une origine purement carienne du *sampi* n'est pas démontrée; exposé prudent chez L. H. Jeffery, *The Local Scripts of Archaic Greece*, 1961, p. 39.

22. Les deux formes Ѱ Ψ existent à Saqqâra. Mêmes formes en lycien pour le *k*, ce qui incite à garder, comme Ševoroškin, cette valeur théorique.[1]

23. Le signe rare en forme d'*oméga* est particulier à Kaunos (15, 16 D).

24. En forme de M posé sur une base, ce signe typique est habituellement considéré comme le *m* du carien, ce qui est assez plausible, comme je l'ai rappelé récemment.[2]

25. Signe très important en carien, quoique plutôt rare à Kaunos, ce caractère a reçu les transcriptions les plus diverses, notamment *ü/w* chez Sayce, *vo* chez Bork-Friedrich, λ (une liquide) chez Ševoroškin.[3] Sans essayer de discuter ces propositions, je laisse ce signe non transcrit.

26. Autre signe très important en carien, employé partout. Mais, à la différence du précédent, il semble que sa valeur soit assurée depuis longtemps comme celle d'un *e*, bref ou très bref. La monnaie lycienne pourvue d'une légende carienne *e–r*, 76 F, fournit un argument de poids en faveur de cette interprétation;[4] noter en outre la ressemblance avec la lettre lydienne ᗡ, où l'on s'accorde à voir une voyelle réduite, notée aujourd'hui *y*.[5]

27 et 28. Ces deux dessins sont évidemment à distinguer. A partir de *27*, je reproduis les signes par les chiffres correspondants, sans essayer de leur donner une valeur, ni de rappeler les propositions anciennes, notamment les transpositions syllabiques utilisée par Bork-Friedrich.

On peut cependant présenter quelques remarques sur *28*.[6] Ce signe n'est pas très répandu à Saqqâra (sept exemples) et ne se trouve pas à Bouhen. Le plus souvent, on lui a attribué une valeur vocalique, depuis *ai*, chez Sayce, jusqu'à *ǝ* ou *i* chez Ševoroškin.[7] Une confirmation intéressante est apportée aujourd'hui par un rapprochement entre des stèles de Saqqâra. D'une part, on a un mot 'court', § 12, 3, *n-g-a-28-k*, en **3** et **9**, et de l'autre, un mot élargi *n-g-a-é-k-h-e*, en **10b**, et **25a**; il s'agit évidemment du même radical, avec *5* ou *é*, en face de *28*.

29 et 30. Ces signes ont été ordinairement distingués l'un de l'autre, avec les valeurs syllabiques *ra* et *ro* chez Bork-Friedrich et Brandenstein. Il m'a paru prudent de les différencier, au moins de manière provisoire: effectivement, une stèle de Saqqâra, **28**, emploie les deux dessins dans le même texte. Pour la présence du second signe, voir aussi **7, 16** (?), **36, 39**. Toutefois, lorsque le dessin de *29* est allongé et aminci vers le bas, on peut hésiter entre les deux schémas: ainsi à Saqqâra, **29**. Ceci pourrait s'expliquer par une identité des deux signes, qui a déjà été postulée par V. Ševoroškin.[8]

31. Ce signe est employé partout.

32. Ce signe est fréquent en Égypte, mais inconnu en Carie (un exemple est cependant apparu en carien de Sardes).[9] A Saqqâra, on trouve surtout ⊓, moins souvent ⊔, parfois ⊏⊐ (**6, 32**), sans doute contamination des deux schémas.

33. Signe généralement rare: en Carie, on le trouve seulement sur une légende monétaire, 18 b D (avec variante 8). Pour l'Égypte, exemples à Abou-Simbel, 75 et 78 Š; sur des stèles de Saqqâra déjà connues, 74 F = **C** M–Y, 46 F = **F** M–Y; enfin, sur une des nouvelles stèles, **22**.

35. Signe rare: pour nos stèles, seulement sur **11**.

[1] Voir aussi Gusmani, op. cit., p. 90 et 94 (no. 10).

[2] *Kadmos* 13 (1974), p. 131–132.

[3] Discussion en dernier lieu chez Gusmani, op. cit., p. 93–94, qui demeure sceptique devant la proposition de Ševoroškin, mais la conserve provisoirement, comme 'Notbehelf'.

[4] *Kadmos* 13 (1974), p. 127–130.

[5] R. Gusmani, *Lydisches Wörterbuch*, 1964, p. 29; cependant, cette lettre est rarement employée, ibid., p. 30, etc.

[6] Ceci résulte d'un échange de vues avec M. Meier. Voir aussi *Kadmos* 16 (1977), p. 93 n. 45.

[7] En dernier lieu, R. Gusmani, op. cit., p. 90 et 93 (valeur *y*).

[8] *RHA* 1964, p. 17 (sans transcription, p. 41 sqq.); *Issledovanija*, p. 112, 191 et passim (transcription par *p*); *Kadmos* 7 (1968), tableau après la p. 172 (id.), etc.

[9] R. Gusmani, *Epichorische Schriftzeugnisse aus Sardis*, p. 90 et 93 (no. 8).

37. Signe inconnu à Saqqâra comme à Bouhen;[1] voir § 6, 2.

38. On a plusieurs exemples à Saqqâra: **1, 4** (aussi variante 王), **24, 28, 34,** etc. Habituellement, on donne à ce signe une valeur consonantique, ainsi *ñ* chez Ševoroškin, *š* chez Gusmani;[2] de nouveaux rapprochements seraient plutôt en faveur d'une valeur vocalique, voir pour **28.**[3]

40. Le signe en forme de flèche, déjà attesté notamment à Abou-Simbel, 77 Š, et à Thèbes, 60 Š, se retrouve à Saqqâra, **5,** et à Bouhen, **50.** Sa transcription demeure problématique.[4]

42. Signe nouveau, spécial à Saqqâra, **26** et **33**; voir § 6, 3.

43. Signe nouveau, sur **9** et **39,** aussi à Bouhen, **50** (et **51**?); voir § 6, 3.

44. Hapax à Saqqâra, **29**; peut-être variante du précédent?

III. Les inscriptions

§ 9, 1. Sur les inscriptions de Bouhen, il n'y a pas grand chose à dire, en l'absence d'un déchiffrement, sinon qu'il s'agit de graffites dont le contenu n'était pas funéraire; plusieurs, **50, 51,** et **55** sont relativement longs, et il doit s'agir de 'souvenirs' laissés par des Cariens de passage, comme à Abou-Simbel. Les autres sont plus ou moins des signatures.

2. Pour ce qui est de Saqqâra, en revanche, il est bien clair que les textes des stèles doivent représenter des épitaphes, en raison du caractère funéraire des monuments. On l'a déjà constaté pour les pièces connues auparavant, et il faut reconnaître que les inscriptions publiées ici n'apportent pas de révélation extraordinaire. Elles sont du même aspect que celles des premières stèles, certains mots s'y retrouvent, d'ailleurs. On peut supposer qu'il y a là des noms, des patronymes, vraisemblablement des ethniques, peut-être des noms de métier.

3. Un problème irritant, mais qui n'est pas nouveau non plus, est celui des rapports éventuels existant entre le texte hiéroglyphique égyptien et le texte carien, sur un tout petit nombre de documents 'bilingues'. Il faut d'abord se demander s'il ne s'agit pas de documents à texte égyptien originel et unique, remployés ultérieurement par un utilisateur carien.[5] La question est d'importance, mais dans notre série, un remploi ne paraît évident que pour une seule stèle, **2**: le texte égyptien, demeuré inachevé, est suivi d'un texte carien, lequel a été, en partie, effacé intentionnellement.[6] La raison de ces tâtonnements nous échappe, mais il est probable qu'on a voulu se servir d'une stèle égyptienne inachevée.

4. Dans le cas d'une belle stèle non décorée, **7,** on a conclu, au contraire, au caractère contemporain des deux textes;[7] cela paraît très vraisemblable, si ce n'est pas absolument démontrable. Mais une première difficulté pour l'interprète moderne vient du fait que l'inscription hiéroglyphique (placée verticalement sous le texte carien) est restée inachevée. Chose plus grave, on n'arrive pas à découvrir une relation entre les trois brèves lignes de carien, fort bien gravées,

---

[1] A propos d'un exemple en carien de Sardes, voir aussi Gusmani, op. cit., p. 91 et 97 (no. 21). Récemment, un exemple est apparu sur un bronze d'Égypte, *Kadmos* 15 (1976), p. 83.

[2] Ševoroškin, *RHA* 1964, p. 24, etc.; de même dans ses publications ultérieures; Gusmani, op. cit., p. 91 et 97 (no. 22).

[3] Ceci sera développé dans une note de M. Meier.

[4] Pour les signes de même forme dans les alphabets épichoriques d'Asie Mineure, voir déjà A. Heubeck, *Lydiaka*, Erlangen, 1959, p. 57–58. Comme on sait, le lycien a une position à part: il s'agit d'une lettre très fréquente, valant *e*;

pour le lydien, valeur consonantique, qui est encore à préciser, cf. Heubeck, op. cit., p. 52–56; R. Gusmani, op. cit., p. 50, transcrit *c*; en vieux-phrygien, signe rare, de valeur encore incertaine, voir M. Lejeune, *Kadmos* 9 (1970), p. 63. Pour le carien même, V. Ševoroškin depuis *RHA* 1964, p. 12–13, etc., rapproche le T et transcrit par un *tau* grec, ce qui ne me paraît pas démontré, voir plus haut pour *18*.

[5] Ce doit être le cas pour la stèle 44 F = *E* M–Y, stèle de donation pour Apriès, qui n'est pas funéraire.

[6] G. T. Martin: 'the Carian text was evidently added later.'

[7] Idem: 'evidently contemporary...'.

évidemment complètes, et la partie existante du texte hiéroglyphique, qui est une généalogie du schéma 'un tel, fils d'un tel, fils d'un tel'. Pourtant, les deux premiers noms, qui sont complets, ne s'expliquent pas comme des noms égyptiens, et doivent en conséquence être considérés comme étrangers, théoriquement comme cariens. Malheureusement (voir le commentaire de **7**), ni 'Iresha' ni 'Nerseker' ne se laissent retrouver dans la partie carienne. Surtout, on ne leur voit pas non plus de correspondants à l'intérieur du répertoire, pourtant abondant, de l'onomastique carienne qui nous est connue par les transcriptions grecques.[1] Il y a donc là un problème qui nous dépasse. Entre autres explications possibles, on peut évidemment avancer que notre transcription, d'ailleurs très partielle, du carien serait totalement fausse, et nous empêcherait de retrouver les noms en question. On peut aussi se demander si l'on a affaire, dans le cas présent, à une véritable bilingue; autrement dit, les textes pourraient différer de contenu, d'une manière ou d'une autre, et le texte carien, sans indiquer la généalogie du défunt, pourrait renfermer seulement des formules funéraires? Mais de telles formules devraient alors se retrouver d'une stèle à l'autre, ce qui n'est pas le cas.

5. Un problème analogue est posé par la stèle **1**. Les deux textes doivent aussi être considérés comme contemporains.[2] Le texte hiéroglyphique, qui est de bonne facture, fournit encore un nom d'homme qui n'est pas égyptien, soit *Mrš* (*ꜣ*) 'Meresha' ou même *Irs* (*ꜣ*) 'Iresha'[3] que nous trouvons déjà sur **7**. Le texte carien, pour sa part, est malheureusement mutilé. Cependant, le premier nom est clair, *a-v-d-e-r-25*, qui est précisément le premier mot de la stèle **7**. Il semble donc exister des coïncidences curieuses entre ces deux stèles, et peut-être une relation entre un mot carien et un nom de la partie hiéroglyphique. Mais, pour le moment, je ne puis en dire davantage.

§ 10. Pour ce qui est de la disposition générale des inscriptions de Saqqâra et de Bouhen, il faut examiner le sens de l'écriture. Comme on l'a remarqué déjà pour le carien d'Égypte, la majorité des textes est sinistroverse: ainsi à Saqqâra, **1–2**, **7–14**, **17–27**, **29**, **31**, **34–36**, **38–40**, **42** et suivants, et à Bouhen, **50–55**. Cependant, les textes dextroverses ne manquent pas à Saqqâra: **3–6**, **15**, **16**, **32**, **33**, **37**. Sur **28**, **30** et **41** on a une double orientation.

§ 11. Suivant l'usage habituel du carien d'Égypte, les mots sont délimités, sur les stèles de Saqqâra, ainsi qu'à Bouhen, par des marques de séparation, dans la mesure où le découpage en lignes ou la position sur la pierre n'indiquent pas déjà la structure des mots. Le procédé le plus fréquent est l'emploi de la barre verticale: ainsi sur **3** (oblique), **4–6**, **8–10**, **12**, **16**, **18**, **20**, **21**, **23**, **24** à **33**, **35**, **38**, **39**, **41**, **43**, **44**; moins fréquent est le point double: **1**, **2**, **13**, **14**, **19**, **22**, **34**, **40**. Pour le découpage en lignes correspondant aux mots, voir **7**, **11**, **37**. A Bouhen, on trouve seulement la barre verticale.

§ 12, 1. Malgré la régularité du procédé de séparation, nous ne rencontrons pas à Saqqâra beaucoup de 'mots' susceptibles de revenir souvent dans le vocabulaire des stèles. Chose étrange, il n'y a même qu'un seul exemple de mot un peu fréquent, celui qui se présente ordinairement comme *n-32-g-o-k-25-h-e*, sur **4**, **5**, **8**, **12**, **20**, **23**, **24**, **27**, **32**, **34**, **38**. Il figure généralement en position finale, **5**, **8**, etc., à une autre place en **4**, **34** et **38**. En outre, il existe aussi sous la forme 'courte', c'est-à-dire sans *h-e* final (plus loin, 3), au moins en **21**; il faut probablement ajouter **6**, avec *n-32-g-o-u-25*, où le *u*, plutôt qu'une variante orthographique, semble être un dessin inachevé de *k* (soit Y pour Ϋ). En tout cas, ce vocable est inconnu à Bouhen, aussi bien que sur les autres sites d'Égypte; ni sa fonction ni son sens n'apparaissent.

---

[1] Voir L. Zgusta, *Kleinasiatische Personennamen*, Prague, 1964, passim.

[2] G. T. Martin: 'the Carian text is exactly contemporary.'

[3] Lecture proposée par J. R. Baines, voir le commentaire de **1**, Part II, p. 59 n. 1.

2. A Saqqâra, j'avais d'abord cru pouvoir isoler un autre mot, moins répandu et plus court, de forme *u-m-27*. Il se trouve, bien délimité, sur **1**, **9**, **14**, **30**, **35**; d'ailleurs, il était déjà attesté sur la stèle du Caire, 44 F = **E** M–Y, après le premier mot. Je crois maintenant qu'il ne s'agit pas d'un mot autonome, mais d'un élément postposé, peut-être d'une combinaison de particules enclitiques (*vel similia*). En effet, *u-m-27* figure régulièrement après un mot qui se termine de la même manière, par le signe *25*. Et surtout, il semble qu'on ait un phénomène analogue avec un 'mot' plus petit, *u-27*, ainsi délimité sur **20**, après un mot à finale en *25*; de même sur **34**, où les 'mots' postposés sont clairement délimités; voir aussi **43**, où le contexte est mutilé. En revanche, sur la stèle déjà connue 48 F = **D** M–Y (qui n'utilise pas de séparateurs), la première séquence se termine par *25-u-27*.[1] Tous ces arguments vont dans le même sens: il doit s'agir de formules postposées. Une seule exception apparente: en **18**, le texte commence par . . .]-*u-25* | *u-m-27-s-a* |. A-t-on, comme variation possible, une formule plus complexe? Ou bien le séparateur serait-il mal placé? Enfin, il existe probablement deux autres formules comparables: d'une part, *32-m-27*, placé aussi, en **28** et **33**, après une séquence terminée en *25*; d'autre part, *u-m-a*, en **5**, qui a la même position.[2]

3. Le texte **34**, dont le lapicide a particulièrement soigné la présentation et le 'découpage' en mots et formules, est, d'autre part, tout à fait démonstratif pour une formule finale, très fréquente, *h-e*, car il montre, à trois reprises, . . .-*25*: *h-e*. Comme on l'avait déjà supposé[3] avant l'apparition de nos stèles, il devient évident que *h-e* est une formule finale postposée, qui est régulièrement (sauf sur **34**) non séparée de ce qui précède. Parfois *h-e*, sans être spécialement délimité, occupe une position un peu à part: ainsi sur **5**, **10b**, **36** (lettres plus petites). Mais, surtout, la formule peut manquer complètement: il s'agit des formes 'courtes', comme celle déjà citée, 2, du type *n-32-g-o-k-25* en face de . . .-*25-h-e*; ajouter *n-k-o-25*, en quatre exemples, **2**, **8**, **19**, **31**, en face de *n-k-o-25-h-e*, **35**; encore *a-v-th-u-th-25* en **36** et . . .-*25-h-e* en **35**. Ceci explique le mot *a-v-n-o-k* en Carie même, à Euromos, 8 D, en face de *a-v-n-o-k-h-e* sur le bronze du Caire, 45 F = **K** M–Y. Il n'y a donc plus de doute qu'on a affaire à une formule postposée, qui joue un rôle important à Saqqâra.[4] Elle était déjà connue en carien d'Égypte, mais avec peu d'exemples: sur des stèles (de Saqqâra), 74 F = **C** M–Y; 43 F = **G** M–Y; sur des bronzes, 45 F déjà cité et 51 F = **M** M–Y; elle est rare sur les graffites, avec un exemple assuré à Abou-Simbel, 77 Š, un autre possible à Bouhen, ici **55** (dernier mot?), mais aucun à Abydos, Thèbes ou Silsile. Enfin, elle semble bien avoir existé en carien de Carie, car la pierre d'Euromos déjà citée, 8 D, a pour premier mot *o-n-o-ḥ-h-e*: (noter la séparation); le même texte fournit, d'autre part, une forme 'courte' *a-v-n-o-k*, mentionnée plus haut.[5] On notera également, en **28**, une formule similaire *h–38*.

§ 13. Il convient enfin d'étudier la 'structure' des inscriptions de Saqqâra. En tenant compte de la place de *h-e* et des finales en *25*, V. Ševoroškin, avec un matériel très réduit, a essayé de dégager certains types.[6] Ainsi la stèle 74 F = **C** M–Y, *th-o-v-l* | *e-s-o-v-25-h-e* | *25-u-33-7-e-25* représenterait pour lui 'Tovl / Sohn von Esova — und / Lyxes', structure A+B *25-h-e*+C *25*; sans la particule, on

---

[1] Peut-être encore une finale *25* | *u-27* sur la stèle de Lausanne, 46 F = **F** M–Y; voir ma réédition ici même, Appendice II.

[2] Une autre séquence de deux signes, *é-38*, est attestée une seule fois, **1**.

[3] Voir *BSL* 68 (1973), p. 196, avec renvoi à des explications de V. Ševoroškin, qui a vu notamment ici une particule de liaison, 'wörterverbindend'. En revanche, on a écarté une proposition de Zauzich, faisant de *h-e* (lu *ir*) un mot qui signifierait 'fils'; idée analogue chez Kowalski, *Kadmos*

14 (1975), p. 75 sqq. (lecture *yr⁰*, sic).

[4] L'index montre une trentaine de mots avec finale *h-e*, presque toujours après une séquence terminée par *25*; bien plus rarement on a . . .-*k-h-e*, **10** et **25**, ou . . .-*7-h-e*, **36**, ou . . .-*29-h-e*, **55**.

[5] En revanche, cette finale ne semble pas se trouver dans les textes en carien de Kaunos; noter en 16 D, ligne 8, la séquence . . .-*t-h-e-r*, mais le contexte général paraît différent.

[6] Voir Ševoroškin dans *RHA* 1964, p. 26–27; *Issledovanija*, p. 207 sqq., etc.; *Kadmos* 3 (1964), p. 77 sqq.

aurait 47 bis F = **B** M–Y, structure A+B *25*+C *25*. Mais l'examen des stèles de Saqqâra montre une situation plus complexe.[1] Pour son type I, on ne peut compter que **22** (où le dernier mot est identique à celui de 74 F), peut-être **39** (si le troisième mot est à compléter en *25*). Pour son type II, on ne retrouve que **6**, avec A+B *25*+C *25*. On pourrait compter ensuite un type III, avec la particule au début, A *h-e*+B *25*+C *25*, ainsi **38** (cf. **40** ?); un type IV, avec en tout deux éléments seulement, A+B *h-e*, ainsi **11**, **15**; un type V, avec la particule en troisième position, A+B *25*+C *h-e*, ainsi **27**, **13**; un type VI, assez fréquent, où la particule occupe la deuxième et la troisième position, A+B *h-e*+C *h-e*, ainsi **5**, **12**, **20**, **23**, **24**, **25**, **32**; ajouter **34**, avec un quatrième élément, D *h-e*. D'autre part, sans la particule, on aurait un type VII, où toutes les finales sont en *25*, structure A *25*+B *25*+C *25* (+D *25*), qui est assez fréquente, **7**, **18**, **21**, **26**, **33**, **19** (ici quatre éléments). On a laissé de côté d'autres structures plus compliquées, dans lesquelles se retrouvent ordinairement *25* et *h-e*, par exemple **35**, de structure A *25*+B *h-e* +C *25*+D *h-e*+E *25*. En conclusion sur ce point, il me paraît donc que les hypothèses de Ševoroškin ne suffisent pas à rendre compte de la variété des structures attestées.

DESSINS ET TRANSLITTÉRATION

L'étude de chaque inscription est accompagnée d'un dessin qui en fournit la reproduction en caractères plus ou moins normalisés, mais non pas complètement uniformisés. Pour un certain nombre de documents, des dessins d'ensemble, en fac-similé, sont donnés à part (Plates XXXI–XXXVIII).

Pour la translittération, les signes de lecture assurée sont représentés par des lettres ou des chiffres en caractères italiques; ces caractères sont pointés lorsque les signes sont mutilés ou effacés, mais en principe reconnaissables. Les signes illisibles sont remplacés par *?* ou par ---. Les restitutions sont placées entre crochets droits. Les séparations de mots indiquées sur la pierre sont marquées par |, /, :, ou un espace.

ABRÉVIATIONS BIBLIOGRAPHIQUES

DEROY ou D = L. DEROY, *Les inscriptions cariennes de Carie, L'Antiquité Classique*, 24 (1955), p. 305–335.

FRIEDRICH ou F = J. FRIEDRICH, *Kleinasiatische Sprachdenkmäler*, Berlin, 1932, VIII, Karische Texte, p. 90–107.

MASSON-YOYOTTE ou M–Y = O. MASSON et J. YOYOTTE, *Objets pharaoniques à inscription carienne*, Le Caire, 1956.

ŠEVOROŠKIN ou Š = V. V. ŠEVOROŠKIN, *Issledovanija po dešifrovke karijskich nadpisej*, Moscou, 1965; transcription des textes cariens p. 308–312, dessins p. 313–319.

ZAUZICH, *Inschriften* = K.-TH. ZAUZICH, *Einige karische Inschriften aus Aegypten und Kleinasien und ihre Deutung nach der Entzifferung der karischen Schrift*, Wiesbaden, 1972.[2]

---

[1] En faisant le décompte des éléments A, B, C, D, etc., je n'ai pas tenu compte des séquences postposées du type *u-m-27*, etc. (§ 12, 2).

[2] Pour une bibliographie complète portant sur la période 1932–1972, voir O. Masson, *BSL* 68 (1973), p. 206–213.

A. INSCRIPTIONS CARIENNES DE SAQQÂRA

I. Stèles cintrées, décorées de motifs égyptiens ou égyptisants

1. H5–1349. A Saqqâra, dépôt des antiquités   Plates I, 1; II, 1; XXXI, 1

Hauteur actuelle 42.3 cm.; largeur 31.3 cm.; épaisseur 8.6 cm.

Calcaire. 'Found in Upper Baboon Gallery, at the junction of the main gallery with the first side gallery.' Campagne 1968–1969.

Stèle cintrée, avec motifs égyptiens, de facture égyptienne; la partie supérieure est seule conservée; description par G. T. Martin, Part II, p. 58–60. Légendes hiéroglyphiques dans les cartouches placés au-dessus des personnages, ainsi que sur une ligne horizontale, au milieu, premier bandeau; au-dessous, dans un bandeau de plus grande dimension, restes de deux lignes en carien, tracées de droite à gauche.

Première reproduction chez W. B. Emery, *JEA* 56 (1970), pl. XV, 5.

Comme le remarque justement G. T. Martin, le texte égyptien et le texte carien, soigneusement disposés, doivent être contemporains; pour l'ensemble, on comparera surtout la stèle dite de Sydney, 43 F = **G** M–Y; disposition différente sur les stèles de Lausanne, 46 F = **F** M–Y, et du Caire, 44 F = **E** M–Y.

Dans le texte hiéroglyphique, deux éléments seulement sont intéressants pour la destination de la stèle. Dans le cartouche horizontal placé devant la figure de l'adorant, à droite, le nom est à lire, soit *Mrš(ꜣ)*, avec G. T. Martin, soit *Ỉrs(ꜣ)*, suivant une ingénieuse proposition de J. R. Baines, citée par G. T. Martin. Dans les deux cas, il s'agirait d'un nom étranger; la seconde lecture permettrait un rapprochement avec le premier nom égyptien de **7**, qui est certainement *Ỉrs(ꜣ)*. Mais aucune de ces formes ne paraît pouvoir se retrouver dans les légendes cariennes.

Dans le cartouche vertical qui est placé au-dessus de la table d'offrande, malheureusement mutilé, G. T. Martin lirait, avec hésitation, . . .*mrymꜣ* (?); on ne voit pas clairement s'il s'agit d'un autre nom, ou d'une indication d'un ordre différent.

Les renseignements fournis par la partie hiéroglyphique sont donc maigres: il s'agit d'un défunt, nommé *Mrš(ꜣ)* ou éventuellement *Ỉrš(ꜣ)*.

Le texte carien est disposé sur deux lignes soigneusement gravées, mais endommagées, surtout la seconde; la direction sinistroverse est évidente.

    (1) *a-v-d-ẹ-r-25: u-m-27: a-v-d-38-ọ*
    (2) *----]-ḥ-e: é-38 | a-ṣ-[--*

L. 1. Le premier mot est presque entièrement conservé; des traces seulement du s. 4, mais le même vocable revient ailleurs, **7** et **43**, avec la même position initiale; en outre, une forme plus courte *a-v-d-e-r* est désormais attestée à Bouhen et à Abydos, voir le commentaire de **50**. La seconde séquence est un élément postposé, assez fréquent à Saqqâra, § 12, 2. Le dernier mot a le même radical que le premier, mais ne se retrouve pas sur nos stèles.

L. 2. Elle est très mutilée; cependant, on constate qu'elle contenait trois séquences, la première terminée probablement par *h-e*. Ensuite une séquence très courte, *é-38*, qui ne revient pas ailleurs; il s'agit apparemment d'un élément postposé, mais les éléments de comparaison manquent.[1] Le dernier mot commençait apparemment par *a-s*.

Cette inscription devrait constituer une bilingue; toutefois, dans l'état actuel de nos connaissances, un rapport entre les deux parties du texte ne peut être décelé, voir § 9, 5.

2. H5–1703 + 1006. A Saqqâra, dépôt des antiquités   Plates I, 2; XXXI, 2

Deux fragments d'une grande stèle, réunis par G. T. Martin: (a) = 1703, hauteur 16 cm., largeur 14 cm., épaisseur 5 cm.; (b) = 1006, hauteur 19 cm., largeur 13 cm., épaisseur 5 cm.

Calcaire. '1703... Found in débris, Sector 3, east of the "South Screen Wall"', campagne 1969–1970; '1006... Found in débris in front of the Entrance of the Baboon Galleries', campagne 1968–1969.

On a deux morceaux de la partie centrale d'une grande stèle, largeur totale environ 26 cm.; description par G. T. Martin, Part II, p. 60–1. On a les restes de deux lignes d'un texte hiéroglyphique; juste au-dessous, restes de deux lignes en carien, allant de droite à gauche.

Ici, comme le montre en détail G. T. Martin, il semble bien qu'on n'a pas affaire à une véritable bilingue, mais à une stèle remployée. En effet, le texte égyptien, qui consiste en une formule funéraire banale, est demeuré inachevé, et ne se poursuit pas sur une troisième ligne. A cette place, on trouve le texte carien, qui a dû être ajouté ultérieurement. Mais, ce qui est curieux et rend la lecture difficile, ces lignes ont été en partie effacées, de manière intentionnelle, dans l'antiquité.

(1) ---ṯ-ḥ-v-n-25 : ṯ-[---]-25-h-e : m-?-u-?-e-25-n-k-o-25
(2) ----?-ṯ-k-ṯ-ḥ-[----]-32-25-o-v-?-25-h-e

Ce texte, assez long, est malheureusement mutilé, avec une lacune au milieu. A la ligne 1, deux séparations marquées par des :, mais ce procédé n'a peut-être pas été employé avec régularité. En effet, dans la partie finale, on est bien tenté de dégager le mot assez fréquent *n-k-o-25*, qui est assuré en **8**, **19** et **31**, voir le commentaire de **8**. On aurait alors devant lui un mot court se terminant par *e-25*.

L. 1. Le premier mot semble avoir une finale en *n-25* (plutôt que *n-th*). Ensuite vient une séquence en *25-h-e* dont le milieu a disparu dans la cassure. J'ai songé, en restituant deux signes, à retrouver ici le radical *ṯ-u-ṯ-25*, qui figure comme tel en **9**, et qui serait une forme 'courte', § 12, 3, mais il y a plutôt la place pour trois signes,[2] ce qui oblige à la prudence. La dernière séquence est probablement à découper en deux parties, comme indiqué ci-dessus. Dans la première, deux signes sont

---

[1] Le voisinage de *é* et de *38* est intéressant, si l'on cherche à reconnaître une voyelle dans le second signe; voir plus haut, § 8, et une étude préparée par M. Meier.

[2] Ceci résulte d'une ultime vérification, faite sur place par M. G. T. Martin (janvier 1977).

très endommagés; cependant, on serait tenté de retrouver *m-g-u-l-e-25*, soit un mot qui est déjà connu à Abydos, fin du graffite 4 F.

L. 2. Le premier mot est très mutilé. Ensuite, lacune d'environ quatre signes. Sur le fragment de gauche, on aurait d'abord *32*, de forme ɯ (plutôt que *38*). Le vocable final, assez long, se termine en *25-h-e*.

3. H5–1229. A Cambridge, Fitzwilliam Museum, E.1. 1971   Plates II, 2; III; XXXII

Hauteur 91.2 cm.; largeur 37 cm.; épaisseur 8 cm.

Calcaire. 'Found as the lining of a pit in the court of Shrine D, Sector 3. The pit contained "Cache no. 2" '; campagne 1968–1969.

Grande stèle cintrée, avec le disque solaire ailé en haut; en dessous, deux personnages, une femme et un homme, debout, face à face, de style non égyptien. Description détaillée par R. V. Nicholls, Part II, p. 61–70. Il n'y a pas de légende hiéroglyphique. En carien, deux lignes incisées du bas vers le haut, parallèlement aux longs côtés.

Premières reproductions: (*a*) W. B. Emery, *JEA* 56 (1970), p. 6 et pl. X, 1; (*b*) R. V. Nicholls, *Archaeological Reports for 1970–1971*, 1971, p. 76 et fig. 13 avec bref commentaire épigraphique par O. Masson.[1]

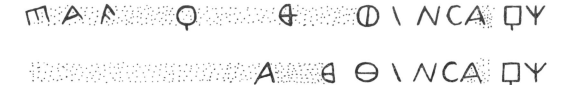

Ce document, unique en son genre, est d'un intérêt exceptionnel, puisqu'il nous montre deux Cariens, ou plutôt deux Caromemphites, une femme et un homme, représentés 'in a kind of provincial East Greek style', vers le milieu du VIe siècle, comme le montre le commentaire approfondi de R. V. Nicholls. Malheureusement, la double inscription carienne est endommagée, surtout dans la partie inférieure de la stèle, et ne peut être lue complètement. En tout cas, il est clair que les deux lignes, soigneusement gravées, ont une direction dextroverse,[2] parallèlement aux longs côtés, du bas vers le haut de la stèle, comme le montrent l'orientation des signes F et C et la structure de l'ensemble; deux barres obliques subsistent comme marques de séparation.

(1) *32-a-v----14-----e---25 \ n-g-a-28-k*
(2) *--------------a-?-e-25 \ n-g-a-28-k*

Il n'y a pas grand-chose à tirer de ce texte. Chaque ligne se termine par le même mot, mais il ne semble pas que les deux lignes aient été identiques.[3] Pour le mot final *n-g-a-28-k*, voir **9** (même position finale). Ce terme est vraisemblablement une forme 'courte', § 12, 3, en face d'une forme élargie en *h-e* qui se rencontre deux fois, *n-g-a-é-k-h-e*, en **10**, *b* et **25**, *a*, car il doit exister une parenté entre le signe *28* et le signe *5* ou *é*, voir § 8.

4. H5–1343. A Londres, British Museum, 67235   Plates IV, 1; XXXIII, 1

Hauteur 62.8 cm.; largeur 30.8 cm.; épaisseur 9 cm.

Calcaire. '...in two fragments. The lower part was found at the foot of the staircase leading into the Lower Baboon Gallery. The upper part was found in the débris in the Lower Baboon Gallery.' Campagne 1968–1969.

---

[1] Autres indications chez R. V. Nicholls, plus loin p. 70.

[2] On devra rectifier ce que j'avais indiqué très provisoirement dans *Arch. Reports*, loc. cit., en supposant à tort une direction sinistroverse (avec début en haut de la stèle).

[3] Le début de chacune est très difficile (pour les traces, le dessin pl. XXXII est peut-être trop optimiste): l. 1, début en *32-a* (ou *32-d*?), finale en *25*; l. 2, début illisible, finale en *a-?-e-25*.

Grande stèle cintrée, avec représentations sur trois registres superposés, les deux premières égyptisantes, la troisième montrant la *prothesis* d'une défunte. Commentaire détaillé par G. T. Martin et R. V. Nicholls, Part II, p. 70–79. Il n'y a pas de légende hiéroglyphique. Sur le bandeau qui sépare les deux registres supérieurs, une ligne de carien, dextroverse, qui se termine à droite en descendant vers le bas.

Première reproduction chez W. B. Emery, *JEA* 56 (1970), pl. X, 2; de là, transcription et essai d'interprétation chez Zauzich, *Inschriften*, p. 18, *L*.

ΛΛ ΗΗΛΓΛΝΙΠⲰΟΙⲞΙΝΠCΟⱲⲰ+θ

▽Γ干ΟΝⲪΙΝ⠿⠿⠿

Le texte est gravé avec régularité, et partout lisible, sauf à l'extrême droite, où le dernier mot est mutilé. L'orientation dextroverse est évidente.

m-38-a-l-v-n | *32-25-0-7-25* | *n-32-g-o-k-25-h-e 29-l-38-o-n-25* | *n-[--*

La scène de *prothesis* qui figure sur le troisième registre montre qu'il s'agit ici de la stèle d'une femme. On ne peut établir si son nom se trouvait indiqué par le premier mot, ou ailleurs.[1] Le troisième mot, en tout cas, est fréquent à Saqqâra, surtout en troisième position, comme ici;[2] voir § 12, 1, etc.

Le premier mot est isolé; le second également, mais sa finale se retrouve en **27**, etc.

Le quatrième mot, s. 20 à 25, est délimité par sa position, sur le bandeau à droite, avec une marque de séparation après *25*. La lecture est évidente; en troisième place, le signe *38*, tracé comme un 干 grec; il n'y a pas lieu de voir ici une variante du type habituel, mais on a un changement d'orientation dû à la position du mot, perpendiculairement au début de l'inscription. Ce terme se retrouve d'ailleurs à Saqqâra, sur **24**, second mot;[3] ce qui est plus notable, il est attesté sur l'un des graffites de Thèbes, 60 Š.[4] Le texte dextroverse se lit: *g-l-e-30-s* | *30-l-38-o-n-25* | *32-g-32-k* | *s-l-l-25-l-25-40*: le second mot est identique, à part l'hésitation, à l'initiale, entre *29* et *30*, § 8. Il y a donc ici un rapprochement remarquable entre ces deux séries de documents, d'autant plus intéressant que de telles rencontres sont rares.

Du dernier mot, il ne subsiste qu'un *n* initial.

5. H5–1228. A Saqqâra, dépôt des antiquités   Plates V, 1; XXXIII, 2

Hauteur 60 cm.; largeur 31.8 cm.; épaisseur 6.4 cm.

Calcaire. Même origine que **3**; campagne 1968–1969.

Grande stèle cintrée, avec représentations sur trois registres superposés, les deux premières égyptisantes, la troisième montrant la *prothesis* d'une défunte. Commentaire détaillé par G. T. Martin et R. V. Nicholls, plus loin, Part II, p. 79–83. Il n'y a pas de légende hiéroglyphique, mais des cartouches correspondants ont été tracés et laissés vides. Sur le bandeau qui sépare le deuxième registre du troisième, une ligne de carien, dextroverse, qui se termine à droite, mais en montant vers le haut (comparer **4**).

---

[1] Selon Zauzich, loc. cit., le nom de la personne défunte figurerait dans le second mot, lu dans sa transcription comme *s-s-o-i-s*, soit le nom égyptien Σισοις. En outre, le troisième mot serait pour lui *ē-s-e-o-u-s-i-r* signifiant 'fils d'Isès'. Ces hypothèses se heurtent à de nombreuses objections.

[2] Le cinquième signe est bien un *k*, et non un V ou *u* comme indiqué chez Zauzich, loc. cit.

[3] Les quatre derniers signes figurent également à la fin du premier mot de **34** (remarque de M. Meier).

[4] Série des graffites découverts en 1951 dans le tombeau de Montouemhat; on peut les citer d'après la numérotation de Ševoroškin, dans son édition provisoire, *RHA* 1964, p. 42–43, et surtout *Issledovanija*, p. 314–315 (petits dessins), p. 310 (transcription). J'ai pu moi-même modifier certaines lectures; voir plus loin, p. 98.

Le texte est assez bien gravé, avec une orientation dextroverse évidente. On relève plusieurs marques de séparation; à ce propos, la répétition du signe *32*, s. 10 et 11, avec des séparations, fait difficulté: aurait-on affaire à une dittographie de cette lettre, au début du mot?

DC↑AQΦIVᗰAIⒸIⒸ□QØ+θINⒸCOY⨀+θ

r-g-40-a-14-25 | u-m-a | 32 | 32-27-14-25-h-e | n-32-g-o-k-25-h-e

Comme dans le cas de la stèle **4**, le défunt devait être une femme, mais nous ne pouvons en dire davantage.

Le premier mot, isolé, est suivi d'une séquence de trois signes, *u-m-a*; c'est un *hapax*, mais du fait de sa structure et de sa position, on est tenté d'y voir une postposition du type *u-m-27*, § 12, 2. Dans le mot initial, noter la présence, s. 3, du signe en forme de flèche, *40*, voir §§ 6, 1 et 8.[1]

Le second mot est isolé;[2] le troisième est fréquent, § 12, 1.

5a. H5–1223. Musée du Caire, JdE 91340   Plates V, 2; XXXIV, 1

Hauteur 44.8 cm.; largeur 29.4 cm.; épaisseur 10 cm.
Calcaire. Même origine que **3**; campagne 1968–1969.
Grande stèle cintrée, analogue à la précédente, avec représentations sur trois registres superposés, les deux premières en style égyptisant, la troisième montrant la *prothesis* d'un défunt. Commentaire détaillé par G. T. Martin et R. V. Nicholls, Part II, p. 83–85.

La stèle ne porte aucune trace d'inscription; comme sur la précédente, des cartouches vides correspondent aux emplacements de légendes hiéroglyphiques. Ainsi que le suppose ingénieusement R. V. Nicholls, il est possible que cette stèle ait porté une inscription carienne peinte, qui aurait complètement disparu. Quoi qu'il en soit, il est indispensable de mentionner ici cette stèle, d'un grand intérêt iconographique.

6. H5–1222. A Saqqâra, dépôt des antiquités   Plates IV, 2; XXXIV, 2

Hauteur 47.6 cm.; largeur 26.5 cm.; épaisseur 6 cm.
Calcaire. Même origine que **3**; campagne 1968–1969.
Stèle cintrée plus simple que les précédentes, avec deux registres seulement, portant des représentations de style égyptisant. Commentaire par G. T. Martin, Part II, p. 85–6. Comme dans les stèles précédentes, les cartouches correspondant à des légendes égyptiennes sont demeurés vides. Au centre, sur un bandeau, une ligne de carien dextroverse, qui se termine à droite en descendant vers le bas.

θ𐊀O□I ᗰθ▽A𐊛NΦIN ⒸCOYθ

---

[1] A propos de la séquence du début, il convient de signaler qu'une légende monétaire, sur une émission de Carie (site inconnu), commence par une séquence *a-40-g*, dans la lecture sinistroverse qui est unanimement adoptée; cf. ma réédition de cette pièce dans *Kadmos* 13 (1974), p. 124–127. Une lecture dextroverse donnerait *g-40-a*, comme ici: elle est peu probable, en raison de l'orientation à gauche du signe *3*, en forme de **C**, et du fait que la seconde partie de la légende, *v-l-e-25*, est indubitablement sinistroverse. Il resterait à supposer une structure en boustrophédon, mais la ressemblance entre les deux documents peut être fortuite; voir également le commentaire de **44**, p. 46.

[2] Si le signe *32*, au début, est répété par erreur, on peut transcrire sous la forme *32-{32}-27-14-25-h-e*, adoptée par commodité dans l'index.

La graphie est assez régulière et l'orientation dextroverse est évidente.

e-v-o-32 | m-e-29-a-v-n-25 | n-32-g-o-u-25

Dans le premier mot, le s. 4 est, à première vue, déconcertant. Mais il est sûr qu'il s'agit d'une variante ou d'une graphie de *32*, de forme 'fermée'; en effet, le signe se rencontre à Saqqâra sous les formes ⊓ (ici même, s. 13) ou bien ⊔; même aspect en **32**, voir § 8. De toute manière, le mot *e-v-o-32*, avec une des formes banales, se retrouve en **8**; voir aussi **19**.

Le second mot doit être comparé avec le second mot de **8**, *ṃ-e-29-v-a-25-h-e*, de structure un peu différente; voir aussi le second mot de **15**, malheureusement mutilé, *a-?-?-e-29-a-v-ṇ-25-h-e*. Ces comparaisons montrent que l'on a ici une forme courte, § 12, 1 et 3; pour une séquence *m-e-29*, voir aussi le début de la stèle 48 F = **D** M–Y.

Le dernier mot est très probablement le terme fréquent à Saqqâra, **4**, **5**, etc., employé sous la forme courte qui est attestée en **21**, c'est-à-dire sans le *h-e* final, § 12, 1 et 3. En effet, vu la ressemblance des signes, il est probable qu'il ne faut pas regarder le *u* comme une variante significative: ce serait plutôt un *k* inachevé, donc Y au lieu de Ψ, et l'on serait en droit de corriger, en lisant *o-(k)-25*.

II. Stèles sans décoration, de type rectangulaire ou cintré

7. H5-1345. Musée du Caire, JdE 91387 Plates VI; XXXV, 1

> Hauteur 43.2 cm.; largeur 29 cm.; épaisseur 7.1 cm.
> Calcaire. Même origine que **1**; campagne 1968–1969.
> Stèle de forme rectangulaire, d'un type qui paraît unique;[1] disposition également originale, avec trois lignes horizontales de carien, en haut, incisées de droite à gauche, et en dessous, deux colonnes d'hiéroglyphes, celle de gauche étant visiblement inachevée. Description et étude du texte hiéroglyphique par G. T. Martin, Part II, p. 86–87.

Il s'agit, malgré sa brièveté relative, d'un des plus beaux documents de Saqqâra, et, sinon d'une véritable bilingue, d'une combinaison de textes ayant un rapport quelconque entre eux: 'both the Carian and the hieroglyphic inscriptions are boldly and deeply incised, and are evidently contemporary' (Martin).

Les trois lignes de carien sont incisées de manière très régulière, avec un tracé large et profond. La direction sinistroverse est évidente; il n'y a pas de marques de séparation, chaque ligne constituant clairement un mot.

(1) *a-v-d-e-r-25*   (2) *u-v-s-h-d-27-25*   (3) *30-e-31-l-s-e-25*

---

[1] Je ne vois pas de pièce identique dans l'ensemble des stèles cariennes découvertes en Égypte. Mais la forme elle-même est assez naturelle; cf. d'ailleurs **41** et **42**, blocs qui pourraient être des stèles rectangulaires grossières.

Comme le montre G. T. Martin, la partie égyptienne du document se lit: 'Iresh(a) fils de Nerseker, fils de Iaḥ-', en admettant que le dernier nom est incomplet, la deuxième colonne d'hiéroglyphes (à gauche) ayant été laissée inachevée par le lapicide.

Étant donné, d'une part, que ces noms, au moins les deux premiers, ne se laissent pas expliquer par l'égyptien, et que, d'autre part, le texte carien fournit précisément trois mots qui ont toute chance de représenter les trois noms d'une généalogie, on s'attendrait à ce que cette symétrie apparente nous permette de retrouver les noms de la partie hiéroglyphique derrière les signes cariens. Malheureusement, il n'en est rien, au moins dans l'état actuel de nos connaissances. Je ne vois pas comment on pourrait rapprocher *Iresh(a)* du premier mot, *a-v-d-e-r-25*, dont on a vu, à propos de **1**, qu'il est attesté trois fois à Saqqâra. Pour le second nom, une comparaison littérale entre *n-r-s-k-r* et *u-v-s-h-d-27-25* ferait apparaître un point de contact avec le *s* en troisième place, mais ensuite? Transcrire Y par *n* et F par *r* ne semble pas spécialement séduisant, sans parler de la fin de chacun de ces mots, qui paraît bien diverger.

En conclusion, ce document nous paraît aussi énigmatique que décevant, tout comme les autres documents où les parties égyptienne et carienne semblent pourtant contemporaines; voir notamment le commentaire de **1**.

8. H5–1014. Musée du Caire, JdE 91386   Plates VII, 1; XXXV, 2

Hauteur 33.5 cm.; largeur 16 cm.; épaisseur 4.8 cm.
Calcaire. 'Found in débris at the entrance to the Baboon Galleries.' Campagne 1968–1969.
Stèle cintrée assez grossièrement taillée; incision formant bordure tout autour. L'inscription carienne n'est pas horizontale par rapport aux petits côtés, mais par rapport aux longs côtés; elle part donc de la base vers le sommet, de droite à gauche.

Les signes ne sont pas gravés très régulièrement, mais sont tous reconnaissables. L'orientation sinistroverse est évidente; les mots sont délimités par des barres de séparation ou par leur position sur la pierre.

(1) *e-v-o-32* | *ṃ-e-29-v-a-25-h-e*   (2) *s-27-n-32-25* | *n-k-o-25*   (3) *n-32-g-o-k-25-h-e*

L. 1. Pour le premier mot, *e-v-o-32*, voir **6**, et aussi **19**. Le s. 5, initiale du second mot, est endommagé dans une cassure; on songerait à un △ ou *d*, mais il s'agit peut-être d'un *m*, si l'on rapproche le second mot de **6**, commençant par *m-e-29*.

L. 2. Il n'y a rien à dire sur le troisième mot. En revanche, le quatrième *n-k-o-25* est intéressant. D'une part, on le retrouve à Saqqâra, en **2**, **19**, et **31**, ainsi qu'en **35**, second mot, élargi en *h-e*, § 12, 3. D'autre part et surtout, il représente un des rares points de contact avec l'épigraphie de la

Carie propre: une épitaphe de Kaunos, 14 D, rédigée dextroverse, a cette forme pour dernier mot, *n-k-o-25*.[1]

L. 3. Le dernier mot est bien connu, § 12, 1.

9. H5-1224. A Londres, British Museum, 67236   Plates VII, 2; XXXV, 3

Hauteur 33.8 cm.; largeur 22.8 cm.; épaisseur 7.8 cm.

Calcaire. Même origine que **3**; campagne 1968–1969.

Stèle cintrée, sans bordure. L'inscription est disposée horizontalement, sur quatre lignes tracées de droite à gauche.

La gravure est très soignée, les signes sont bien conservés; les s. 1 et 2 avaient été effacés et ont été regravés. Orientation sinistroverse évidente; les mots sont délimités par leur disposition, une marque de séparation, ou rien (l. 3).

(1) *r-a-v-k-a-e-25*   (2) *u-m-27 | th-u-th-25*   (3) *43-27-n-25-h-e-n-g*   (4) *a-28-k*

L. 1. Le mot initial est isolé, mais on a déjà des mots commençant par *r-a-v*, par exemple dans **22**, et ailleurs en carien d'Égypte, index B; voir aussi **14**, commentaire.

L. 2. On a d'abord la formule *u-m-27*, qui se rattache au terme précédent, voir § 12, 2. Ensuite, la séquence *th-u-th-25* constitue certainement un mot indépendant; il a l'aspect d'une forme 'courte', § 12, 3, comme un mot de structure similaire qui apparaît en **36**, avec un début en *a-v*, à côté du terme correspondant à finale *h-e*, en **35**.

L. 3–4. En dépit de l'absence de séparation, il est clair qu'il faut distinguer deux mots: d'abord, s. 15 à 20, avec finale en *h-e*, et s. 21 à 25, un terme déjà fourni par **3**, avec la même position finale; à ce sujet, voir le commentaire de **3**. L'avant-dernier mot est donc *43-27-n-25-h-e*, avec à l'initiale le signe rare *43*, employé seulement à Saqqâra et à Bouhen, § 8.

10. H5-1225. Musée du Caire, JdE 91385   Plates VIII, 1; XXXV, 4

Hauteur 35.5 cm.; largeur 22.8 cm.; épaisseur 6 cm.

Calcaire. Même origine que **3**; campagne 1968–1969.

[1] Ševoroškin, *Issledovanija*, p. 311, 98 Š, propose aussi de le retrouver à la fin d'une inscription mutilée d'Euromos, *n-k-o-[25]*. Enfin, dans le texte de Tasyaka, 15 D, on voit la même séquence à la ligne 3 (les mots ne sont pas séparés; Ševoroškin, op. cit., p. 312, suppose un mot *sl-nko25-29*).

Stèle cintrée, avec bordure et fronton évidé. Une première inscription de cinq lignes (*a*), gravée horizontalement, occupe presque toute la surface; en dessous, inscription de trois lignes (*b*) évidemment rajoutée dans l'espace libre; le tout gravé de droite à gauche.

Les deux inscriptions sont gravées de manière très différente: la première avec des lettres épaisses mais irrégulières, contenant des traces de couleur rouge; la seconde avec des lettres grêles, rapidement incisées.[1] Les deux textes doivent être indépendants: autre situation sur **25**, où la même légende est partiellement répétée. L'orientation sinistroverse est évidente.

(*a*) (1) *14-a-r-u-l-14-25*   (2) *29-u-a-v-e-25-l*   (3) *a-v | 25-27-k*
     (4) *k-e-th-a-u-25*   (5) *m-14-k-u-m-e*
(*b*) (1) *e-g-n-u-o-k-25*   (2) *h-e | n-g-a-é-k*   (3) *h-e*

(*a*) L. 1. Le premier mot est isolé.

L. 2–3. Il est très probable que le mot de la l. 2 se termine avec *a-v*, l. 3; on obtient alors un deuxième mot de neuf lettres.

L. 3–4. Faute de parallèles, on ne voit pas clairement s'il y a ici un autre mot long occupant presque deux lignes, s. 17 à 25, ou plutôt deux mots, suivant la coupe des lignes, s. 17–19 et 20–25. Le signe 25, plus petit et grêle, semble avoir été rajouté en fin de ligne.

L. 5. Un dernier mot *m-14-k-u-m-e*; cette séquence fait penser à un graffite d'Abydos, 20 F, second mot, copié par Sayce comme *m-14-k-u-?-r*, mais il n'a pas été retrouvé en 1956 pour révision; encore à Abydos, comparer le début de 2 *b* F, *m-14-k-*...

---

[1] 'The first five lines are deeply incised and bear traces of red pigment. The remaining three lines (and the last sign, line 4) are roughly scratched in another hand. No trace of pigment on these signs' (note des fouilleurs). Pour la présence de couleur dans les signes, voir aussi **19, 45**. Sur ce procédé, bien connu en Grèce, en Égypte, etc., remarques et bibliographie chez J. et L. Robert, *Rev. Ét. Gr.* 87 (1974), *Bull. Épigr.* no. 692.

(*b*) La structure du second texte est claire: deux mots à finale *h-e*. Le premier mot, commençant par *e-g-n-u-*, fait songer au premier mot de **25**, *a*, *e-g-n-k-s*. Dans le second mot, des lectures incertaines à première vue, A à barre horizontale peu visible et E ou *é* à trois branches tournées vers le bas, sont confirmées par la présence du même mot sur **25**, *a* en position finale. Pour ce second mot, voir le commentaire de **3**.

Malgré sa longueur, le double texte de cette stèle est tout à fait obscur: comme il a été indiqué plus haut, on n'aperçoit pas de relation entre les deux inscriptions.

11. H5-1404. A Londres, University College, 2405   Plate VIII, 2

Hauteur 30.5 cm.; largeur 21 cm.; épaisseur 11.5 cm.
Calcaire. 'Found in the débris of the Upper Baboon Gallery'; campagne 1968–1969.
Stèle cintrée sans bordure; deux lignes horizontales, gravées de droite à gauche.

Gravure régulière; orientation sinistroverse évidente.

(1) *m-k-u-25-o-7*   (2) *35-n-u-25-h-e*

L. 1. Le premier mot a une finale en *25-o-7*, comparer **16, 22**.
L. 2. Le second mot commence par le signe rare *35*: pas d'autre exemple à Saqqâra.

III. Stèles du type 'fausse-porte'

12. H5-1344. Musée du Caire, JdE 91384   Plate IX, 1

Hauteur 29.1 cm.; largeur 19.6 cm.; épaisseur 7 cm.
Calcaire. Même origine que **1**; campagne 1968–1969.
Texte disposé sur l'encadrement extérieur, de droite à gauche, commençant à droite, à 7 cm. de la base.
Première reproduction par W. B. Emery, *JEA* 56 (1970), pl. XV, 4 (petite photographie inversée au tirage); d'où transcription chez Zauzich, p. 19–20, *N*.

Inscription bien gravée, avec de grands signes; orientation sinistroverse.

u-th-s-e | *r-v-32-d-e-25-h-e* | *n-32-g-o-k-25-h-e*

Trois mots, dont le dernier est le mot fréquent en finale, sous sa forme la plus courante, § 12, 1, les autres étant isolés.[1]

13. H5-1347. Musée du Caire, JdE 91373   Plates IX, 2; XXXVI, 1

Hauteur 33 cm.; largeur 21.6 cm.; épaisseur 7.6 cm.
Calcaire. Même origine que **1**. Campagne 1968–1969.

---

[1] Comme dans les autres cas, il n'y a rien à tirer de l'interprétation pseudo-grecque de Zauzich, loc. cit.

Texte disposé sur deux lignes: dans l'encadrement extérieur, puis dans l'encadrement intérieur; direction de droite à gauche, début de chaque ligne en haut à droite.

ΦΩΨΝΟΜ : ΦΙΟΦΠΨΥΛ

Θ+ΦΘΜΔ٦ϙ⊕

Gravure très soignée, lettres assez profondes et grandes. L'orientation sinistroverse est évidente.

(1) *m-u-k-32-25-o-7-25* : *s-o-n-k-27-25*   (2) *th-28-l-d-s-e-25-h-e*

Le premier mot est isolé.[1] Le second se retrouve sur **26**, également comme second terme d'un texte de trois mots. Le troisième mot, avec le signe rare *28*, est isolé.

13a. H5-1348. A Londres, University College, 2407

Hauteur 32.5 cm.; largeur 22.5 cm.; épaisseur 6.5 cm.
Calcaire. Même provenance.

Cette stèle n'a pas été incisée, mais montre seulement des traces très faibles d'inscription à l'encre noire, sur les montants verticaux; aucune lettre n'est reconnaissable.

14. H5-1350. A Cambridge, Fitzwilliam Museum, E.3.1971   Plate X, 1

Hauteur 42.5 cm.; largeur 20.5 cm.; épaisseur 7.3 cm.
Calcaire. Même origine que **1**.
Stèle très haute, brisée en deux morceaux; le côté gauche est endommagé, et il ne subsiste que le début du texte, une ligne horizontale sur l'encadrement extérieur, gravée de droite à gauche.
Mention par R. V. Nicholls, *Archaeological Reports for 1970-71*, p. 76 (sans reproduction).

▨▨▨ : ΩΛΥ : ΦϟΑϙ٦Α

Gravure très soignée, orientation sinistroverse évidente. Il ne subsiste du texte que deux séquences.

a-v-14-a-é-25 : *u-m-27* : [-----

Malgré sa brièveté, cette inscription est intéressante. On a une séquence de six lettres, suivie de la formule postposée *u-m-27*, § 12, 2. Or, une structure comparable figure en **9**, avec un mot initial très ressemblant. Le rapprochement avec *r-a-v-k-a-e-25* fait ressortir trois points: d'abord, la présence ou l'absence du *r*- initial; en second lieu, l'équivalence entre *e* et *é* devant *25*, § 8. Enfin, on remarquera que le signe *14*, sur cette stèle, correspond à *k* sur **9**, ce qui paraît bien indiquer pour *14* une valeur telle que *q*, § 8.

15. H5-1351. A Londres, British Museum, 67251   Plate X, 2

Hauteur 34 cm.; largeur 18.8 cm.; épaisseur 6 cm.
Calcaire. Même origine que **1**.

---

[1] Cependant, les cinq derniers signes forment un mot indépendant sur **4**, et se retrouvent, dans une autre combinaison, sur **27** (remarque de M. Meier).

Stèle très endommagée dans la partie supérieure. Le texte est disposé comme sur deux lignes: la première occupe la corniche; la seconde commence à gauche de la partie horizontale de l'encadrement extérieur et se termine en descendant vers la droite, allant donc de gauche à droite. Au-dessus de la porte, motif en forme de bouton de lotus (cf. **37**).

Gravure assez irrégulière; certains signes semblent avoir été regravés. La direction dextroverse est évidente (avec F, N tournés à droite).

(1) *a-m-?-?-?-32-s*   (2) *a-?-?-e-29-a-v-n̠-25-h-e*

Le premier mot, en *a-m*, est isolé, et ce début paraît rare, comparer *a-m-n-27-k* dans **36**. La seconde séquence est particulièrement longue; elle correspond en grande partie au second mot de **6**, qui commence par *m-e-29*, mais ne comporte pas la finale *h-e*.[1]

16. H5-1352. A Cambridge, Fitzwilliam Museum, E.2.1971   Plate XI, 1

Hauteur préservée 26.8 cm.; largeur 20 cm.; épaisseur 6 cm.
Calcaire. Même origine que **1**.
Stèle endommagée dans sa partie inférieure. La disposition du texte est la même que sur la stèle précédente, avec une première ligne sur la corniche et une seconde sur l'encadrement extérieur, se continuant à droite en descendant vers le bas, donc de gauche à droite.
Mention par R. V. Nicholls, *Archaeological Reports for 1970–71*, p. 76.

Gravure assez soignée. Orientation dextroverse évidente.

(1) *14-g-u-25-o-7*   (2) *30-l-o-s | r-a-n-s-th-e-[?*

Le premier mot a une finale en *25-o-7*, comme en **11**. Au début du second mot, soit *29*, soit plutôt *30* (petite haste en bas); noter le *l* qui a la forme d'un lambda grec à branches égales; mot court à finale en *-o-s*, comme en **37**.[2] Le dernier mot est probablement incomplet.

17. H5-1353. Musée du Caire, JdE 91383   Plate XI, 2

Hauteur 32.3 cm.; largeur 21.5 cm.; épaisseur 7.3 cm.
Calcaire. Même origine que **1**.
Stèle endommagée à l'angle supérieur droit. Le texte est disposé symétriquement sur l'encadrement extérieur, de droite à gauche; début en bas, à droite.

---

[1] Remarque faite par M. Meier.
[2] Le radical, isolé à Saqqâra, semble bien se retrouver à Thèbes, 48 Š, avec le mot *30-l-o-30-14-25*.

Gravure irrégulière, un peu tremblée; orientation sinistroverse évidente.

$$A \bowtie I \oplus B \ddagger \mathsf{1} \mathsf{1} A D \quad \cdots \quad B \bowtie A B \exists$$

$$B + \oplus \mathsf{N} \exists \Box \bowtie \mathsf{1}$$

é-e-a-s-e-?-?-r-ạ-é-v-e-th | m-a-v-m-27-é-n-25-h-e

Dans la première séquence, il y avait probablement deux mots, le second pouvant commencer avec le *r*, à l'angle supérieur droit; on a des mots commençant par *r-a*. Quant au premier mot, il a comporté sept ou huit signes; noter le début curieux en *é-e-a*, cf. en **38**.

Le dernier mot est parfaitement lisible. Il ne se retrouve pas à Saqqâra, mais il rappelle de manière notable le mot qui est connu depuis longtemps sur l'Apis en bronze du Caire, 45 F = **K** M–Y, sur lequel on lit (dextroverse) d'une part *m-a-v-a-27-é-n*, de l'autre *m-a-v-8-27-é-n*. Ainsi, on aurait presque le même mot, élargi à Saqqâra par une finale *25-h-e*, s'il n'y avait en plus, encore à Saqqâra, un *m* en quatrième place. La raison de ces variations nous échappe, mais il est intéressant de trouver cette rencontre entre le vocabulaire des objets votifs et celui des stèles de Saqqâra.[1]

18. H5–1354. A Londres, British Museum, 67252   Plate XII, 1

Hauteur 33 cm.; largeur 21 cm.; épaisseur 4.8 cm.
Calcaire. Même origine que **1**.
Stèle endommagée et reconstituée à l'aide de plusieurs fragments. Disposition inhabituelle: le texte doit commencer en haut à droite, sur la partie horizontale de l'encadrement extérieur et se poursuit sur la partie gauche vers le bas de la stèle, donc de droite à gauche.

$$\oplus B \bowtie \mathsf{1} \mathsf{V} I \oplus \triangle \Box B \dashv \varphi I A \mathsf{M} \Box \mathsf{M} Y I \oplus Y \cdots$$

Gravure assez irrégulière. Le texte étant lacunaire en haut à droite, le début de l'inscription manque; orientation sinistroverse.

-----u-25 | u-m-27-s-a | 14-v-e-27-d-25 | n-v-s-e-25

Le premier mot se termine par *u-25*. Le second paraît être la formule *u-m-27*, exceptionnellement élargie par *s-a*, § 12, 2. Le troisième mot est isolé. Le quatrième et dernier *n-v-s-e-25* est déjà connu pour le dernier mot d'une stèle fausse-porte de Memphis-Saqqâra, 47 bis F = **B** M–Y;[2] c'est sans doute un trait qui souligne une commune origine possible pour ces documents.[3]

---

[1] J'ai déjà attiré l'attention sur ce point dans *Kratylos* 18 (1973), p. 40, en critiquant une suggestion de Zauzich, p. 10, qui voudrait voir sur le bronze chaque fois un M final (pour lui de valeur *m*) au lieu du N dextroverse que donnent les éditions (cf. Masson–Yoyotte, *Objets*, p. 43, fig. 21). Cette lecture évidente est confirmée par la présence du N (ici orienté à droite) sur la stèle de Saqqâra. Mais — ce qui est un point accessoire ici — je ne crois plus à la distinction entre *n* et *vu* que j'avais soutenue dans *Kratylos*; voir Introduction, § 8.

[2] O. Masson, *RHA* xii (1953), p. 34–35 et pl. XIII; Masson–Yoyotte, *Objets*, p. 4–6; sur la fig. 5, le dernier signe a été dessiné par erreur comme *o* au lieu de *25*, mais voir la fig. 4 et la transcription.

[3] L'interprétation de ce mot par Zauzich, p. 21–22, avec une lecture *ē-t-s-r-s*, comme valant un verbe pseudo-grec ἐστήρισε 'hat (die Stele) aufgestellt', est particulièrement invraisemblable, cf. O. Masson, *Kratylos* 18 (1973), p. 41.

19. H5–1355. A Oxford, Ashmolean Museum, 1971.106   Plate XII, 2

Hauteur 34.4 cm.; largeur 24.5 cm.; épaisseur 6.5 cm.

Calcaire. Même provenance que **1**.

Stèle endommagée et reconstituée à l'aide de fragments. La disposition des mots est inhabituelle. Il faut distinguer deux parties: (i) sur la corniche supérieure et en haut de l'encadrement extérieur gauche, signes assez profonds, avec des traces de couleur noire, de droite à gauche; (ii) verticalement sur l'encadrement extérieur de droite, mais la base des signes vers l'extérieur; le début est donc en haut à droite, texte gravé plus légèrement et sans couleur, même orientation.

On peut disposer l'inscription sur deux lignes, sinistroverses.

(1) *e-v-o-32-25 : m-s-t-28-n-?-25*
(2) *m-14-14-u-25 : n̞-k-o-25*

L. 1. Le premier mot est déjà connu dans **6** et **8**, *e-v-o-32*. Dans le second mot, remarquer la présence du signe T ou *18*, qui n'est pas fréquent.

L. 2. Dans le premier mot, on notera la répétition *14-14*, qui est déjà connue sur une stèle de Saqqâra, **47** F = **A** M–Y.[1] Le second mot est assuré, bien que la première lettre se trouve dans une cassure: en effet, c'est le terme connu *n-k-o-25*, voir le commentaire de **8**.

20. H5–1356. Musée du Caire, JdE 91372   Plates XIII, 1; XXXVI, 2

Hauteur 38.5 cm.; largeur 20.3 cm.; épaisseur 6.8 cm.

Calcaire. Même provenance que **1**.

Belle stèle, presque intacte. Le texte commence en haut, à droite, sur l'encadrement extérieur, et se poursuit sur l'encadrement de gauche; seconde ligne sur la partie horizontale de l'encadrement intérieur, de droite à gauche.

On peut disposer l'inscription sur deux lignes sinistroverses.

(1) *s-a-k-u-th-25 | u-27 | m-k-14-n-u-k-25-h-e*
(2) *n-32-g-o-k-25-h-e*

L. 1. Le premier mot, commençant par *s-a-k*, fait penser au second mot de la bilingue d'Athènes, **19** D, *s-a-k-14-u-v-*[. Ensuite, on a la petite séquence *u-27*, bien délimitée par les barres de séparation, comme en **34** (après le premier mot) et en **43**; il doit s'agir d'une formule postposée du même type que *u-m-27*, voir la discussion, § 12, 2.

---

[1] Séquence ?/*14-14-l-a-35-e-*[*25*], peut-être un mot complet, si l'on compare deux graffites d'Abydos qui commencent par *14-14*, voir index B.

Le mot suivant est isolé; comparer éventuellement le début en *m-g-14*, sur **51**.[1]

L. 2. Le dernier mot est fréquent à cette place, § 12, 1.

21. H5–1357. Musée du Caire, JdE 91382   Plate XIII, 2

Hauteur 33.8 cm.; largeur 20 cm.; épaisseur 7.5 cm.

Calcaire. Même provenance que **1**.

Stèle endommagée à droite. Le texte est disposé symétriquement sur l'encadrement extérieur, de droite à gauche.

NI ⊕Ɗ∃ON□∨∃I ⊗ ⊗I⊕ϙ□ ⊗ ⋇M

⊕Ψ○⊃ᙀ

Graphie irrégulière, signes plus ou moins espacés; le début, à droite, est endommagé; orientation de droite à gauche.

ṣ-?-?-27-14-25 | ?-? | é-k-27-n-o-v-ẹ-25 | n-32-g-o-k-25

Le premier mot, avec des lettres très espacées, semble avoir comporté six signes, avec un petit M peu lisible au début; ensuite une séquence de deux signes, probablement une formule postposée du type *u-27*, etc.; du second signe il reste une haste verticale.

Le troisième mot, avec des espacements variables, est clair; même finale qu'en **40**.

Le dernier mot est le terme fréquent en finale, mais sous sa forme courte, § 12, 1 et 3.

22. H5–1358. Musée du Caire, JdE 91381   Plate XIV, 1

Hauteur 40 cm.; largeur 24.6 cm.; épaisseur 8 cm.

Calcaire. Même provenance que **1**.

Stèle endommagée à gauche, mais le texte est intact. Le début occupe la partie horizontale de l'encadrement supérieur et se continue sur l'encadrement intérieur, donc de droite à gauche.

I○⊕Ψ↗ＡƊ

⊕ƀI⅄Ψ⊙:ƀ+⊕⊕□IM

Signes assez profondément incisés, mais irréguliers.

(1) *r-a-v-u-25-o-7*   (2) *m-7-27-th-25-h-e : 25-u-33-7-e-25*

L. 1. Le mot initial est intéressant. Des parallèles dans les graffites d'Égypte montrent que le s. 1 est bien un *r* ou *15*, panse à droite, et surtout que le s. 3, malgré sa forme de flèche, est un F maladroit, tourné à gauche. En effet, on retrouve exactement le même mot *r-a-v-u-25-o-7* à Abydos, 4 F (après révision de la copie inexacte de Sayce), et encore en Nubie, 72 F, graffite du Gebel Sheik

---

[1] Voir *Kadmos* 16 (1977), p. 92–93.

Suleiman, second mot (la copie de Sayce est ainsi confirmée).[1] Il en résulte une rencontre notable entre trois sites différents.

L. 2. Le second mot est isolé. En revanche, le troisième, où figure le signe rare *33*, est déjà connu sur des stèles apparues au XIXᵉ s., sur 74 F = C M–Y et sur 46 F = F M–Y, ici avec une variante finale, *th* ou *9* au lieu de *25*; malgré la ressemblance entre *9* et *25*, il n'y a pas à corriger.[2]

23. H5-1359. Musée du Caire, JdE 91380 Plate XIV, 2

Hauteur 35 cm.; largeur 21.7 cm.; épaisseur 7.2 cm.
Calcaire. Même provenance que **1**.
Stèle endommagée à gauche. Le texte est disposé sur l'encadrement intérieur, avec début en haut, à droite, donc de droite à gauche.

ⵔⵏⵟⵏⵕⴰⴰⵉⵟⵉⵕⵊⵟⵕⵘⵥⵢⵘ

ⵟ⵶ⵕⵥⵕⵊⵘⵏⵉⵊⵜ

Gravure très régulière. La fin de l'inscription est endommagée, mais peut être complétée.

32-k-u-14-e-25 | 29-32-a-v-25-n-t-n-25-h-e | n-32-g-o-k-25̣-[h]-e̦

Le premier mot est isolé. Le second également; il est remarquable par sa longueur, avec onze signes. Au début, probablement *29*, sans haste inférieure (qui indiquerait *30*); noter la présence du T ou *18*; trois fois N dextroverse, malgré l'orientation à gauche.

Le dernier mot est courant à Saqqâra, § 12, 1.

24. H5-1360. A Birmingham, City Museum, 68, 71 Plate XV, 1

Hauteur 35.5 cm.; largeur 20 cm.; épaisseur 7 cm.
Calcaire. Même provenance que **1**.
Stèle endommagée et reconstituée, mais le texte est pratiquement intact, disposé sur l'encadrement extérieur, de droite à gauche; début à droite.

ⵟⵝⵉⵕⵎⵕⵟⵗⵉⵟⵉⵟⵘⵕⵊⵢⵕⵟ

ⵟⵝ ⵕⵥⵕⵕⵘⵏⵉⵢⵕ

Signes régulièrement incisés, de belle facture.

e-14-u-v-o-32-25 | 29-l-38-o-n-25 | h-e-27-k | n-32-[g]-o-k-25-h-e

---

[1] On sait que ce remarquable graffite est le témoignage le plus méridional de l'activité des Cariens en Égypte, § 4. Il est regrettable qu'il n'ait pas été photographié en ces dernières années, avant d'être submergé par les eaux du Nil: on le connaît seulement par la copie de Sayce, 72 F, et par un relevé rapide d'A. J. Arkell (en ma possession), cf. Arkell, *JEA* 36 (1950), p. 27; ce relevé a été utilisé par Ševoroškin,

Issledovanija, p. 147 sq. et 311, 316, 85 Š. Le second mot, qui est sûr, se retrouve ici; en outre, le quatrième mot revient, en tout ou en partie, sur la stèle **30**.

[2] Le mot *25-u-33-7-e-25*, lu comme λυχzeλ, joue un rôle important dans le déchiffrement de Ševoroškin, qui y voit une forme correspondant au nom carien Λυξης, Lyxès: voir *Nestor*, 1963, p. 282–283, et *Issledovanija*, p. 182, 329, etc.

Le premier mot fait penser à *e-v-o-32-25*, dans **19**.

Le second mot est déjà connu par **4**, et à Thèbes; voir le commentaire. Un problème est posé par le quatrième mot, *h-e-27-k*; on s'attendrait à ce que *h-e* soit coupé autrement, et rattaché au mot précédent; mais alors, que ferait-on de *27-k*? serait-ce une formule postposée?

Le dernier mot est le terme final usuel à Saqqâra, § 12, 1.

25. H5–1361. Musée du Caire, JdE 91379   Plate XV, 2

Hauteur 28.5 cm.; largeur 18.7 cm.; épaisseur 6.5 cm.
Calcaire. Même provenance que **1**.
Texte en partie double, avec une disposition originale: (1) partie horizontale et montant gauche de l'encadrement extérieur; (2) sur deux lignes horizontales, dans le rectangle placé au-dessus de la 'porte', le tout de droite à gauche.

Ɓ + ᕦ ᔨ A) N I Ɓ + ⊕ ⊡ ᔨ ᔨ N I M ᕦ N) Ɓ

Ɓ + ⊖ ⊡ ᔨ ᔨ ᒲ I M ᕦ N) Ɓ

Le texte est répété partiellement; la gravure et la forme des lettres indiquent une même main, et l'on ne voit pas la raison de cette disposition.

(*a*) *e-g-n-k-s* | *n-é-v-27-25-h-e* | *n-g-a-é-k-h-e*
(*b*) *e-g-n-k-s* | *n-é-v-27-25-h-e*

Pour le premier mot, on peut rapprocher **10**, *b*, *e-g-n-u-o-k-25*; le second est isolé. Le troisième mot se retrouve aussi sur **10**, *b*, avec la même forme exactement; sur cette séquence, voir le commentaire de **3**.

On peut noter que tous les *n* ont la forme N, dextroverse, malgré l'orientation à gauche du texte, sauf le dernier de forme ᒲ.

26. H5–1362. Musée du Caire, JdE 91378   Plates XVI, 1; XXXVI, 3

Hauteur 37 cm.; largeur 26.9 cm.; épaisseur 7.6 cm.
Calcaire. Même provenance que **1**.
Stèle en assez bon état. Le texte est disposé sur l'encadrement intérieur, avec début à droite, allant de droite à gauche.
Première publication par W. B. Emery, *JEA* 56 (1970), pl. XV, 2; d'où Zauzich, p. 19, *M*.

⊕ ⠶ A φ A + Ꮾ φ I ⊕ ⊡ ᕦ ᒲ O M I ⊕ Ꮾ ⊡ ᒲ

Gravure fine mais précise, grandes lettres. On notera, s. 3 et 12, la présence de la lettre très rare *42*, en forme de 6; cf. **33** et voir §§ 6 et 8.

n-27-42-25 | *s-o-n-k-27-25* | *14-42-h-a-14-a-[v]-25*

Le premier mot est isolé. Le second est déjà connu par **13**, avec la même position. Le troisième se retrouve sur **33**, avec la même position, ce qui permet de suppléer ici un *v* pour l'avant-dernière lettre, disparue dans une cassure.

27. H5–1401. Musée du Caire, JdE 91377   Plate XVI, 2

Hauteur 33 cm.; largeur 22 cm.; épaisseur 6.5 cm.

Calcaire. Même provenance que **11**.

Stèle de dessin très simplifié. Le texte commence sur la partie horizontale de l'encadrement et se continue sur le montant de gauche.[1]

$$I \; \Phi I \; O \; \oslash III \;) \; I \; M \; \triangle \; \dashv \Delta \; O \; \varphi \; \curlyvee$$

$$\dashv + \Phi \; \curlyvee \; O \;) \; III \; N$$

Graphie très irrégulière, avec des signes couchés; en outre, le s. 4, quoique très net, est d'interprétation incertaine: est-ce un △ ou *d*, avec un élément indûment prolongé vers le haut, ou bien un signe *30* à l'envers?

k-14-o-d (ou *30*?)-*v-e-s* | *g-32-25-o-7-25* | *n-32-g-o-k-25-h-e*

Le premier mot est isolé; finale rare en *e-s*.

Le second mot, avec en plus le *g* initial, correspond au second mot de **4**, *32-25-o-7-25*; voir aussi **13**. Le troisième est le mot final usuel, § 12, 1.

28. H5–1434. Musée du Caire, JdE 91376   Plate XVII, 1

Hauteur 35 cm.; largeur 20.2 cm.; épaisseur 7.5 cm.

Calcaire. Provenance: 'Upper Baboon Gallery, in the débris of the first side gallery.'

Belle stèle, presque intacte. Disposition très symétrique sur l'encadrement intérieur, mais l'orientation ne se détermine pas à première vue.

Première publication par Emery, *JEA* 56 (1970), pl. XV, 1; d'où Zauzich, p. 20–21, *O*.

$$I \; \oplus \; A \; F \; M \; M \; \theta \; \Phi$$

$$\text{H} + \Phi \; \dashv \; O \; \curlyvee \; \triangle \; I \; \square \; M \; \sqcap \; I \; \Phi \; V \; M \; M \; \triangledown \; \sqcap$$

Belle inscription, avec des caractères soigneusement gravés. D'après la disposition habituelle, on s'attendrait à un début en bas, à droite, donc à une lecture sinistroverse de l'ensemble. Mais cette orientation ne doit être acceptée qu'à partir du second mot, placé horizontalement: elle donnerait des séquences inattendues pour le premier mot, à droite. En outre, on constate que le F du premier mot est orienté à droite: il est donc clair que ce mot a été gravé dextroverse, contrairement au reste.[2]

th-a-v-m-s-e-25 | *32-29-s-n-u-25* | *32-m-27* | *d-30-o-v-25̣-h-38*

Le premier mot rappelle une forme analogue *th-a-v-s-e-25̣* sur une des stèles déjà connues de Saqqâra, 48 bis F = **H** M–Y; cette comparaison montre que la dernière lettre de ce document est

---

[1] Près de la base, au milieu de la fausse-porte, traces de couleur, en rouge et en noir, et peut-être traces de lettres (illisibles).

[2] Il est inutile de discuter ici l'interprétation donnée par

Zauzich pour ce texte (avec des éléments pseudo-grecs), d'autant plus que sa transcription, faite à partir de la photographie du *JEA*, contient des erreurs de détail, et surtout une lecture sinistroverse du premier mot, qui nous paraît exclue.

bien un signe *25* endommagé, et non pas un *o*, comme l'a vu déjà V. Ševoroškin.[1] En définitive, les deux vocables ne diffèrent que par l'insertion' d'un *m* au milieu, dans la présente forme ; peut-on comparer le cas de **17** ?

On a ensuite un mot terminé par *25* et suivi par une séquence de trois signes, *32-m-27*, qui se retrouve, dans une situation analogue, sur **33** ; étant donné sa position et sa structure, il est bien probable qu'il s'agit d'une formule postposée, comparable à la formule plus courante *u-m-27*, § 12, 2. Le second mot lui-même est notable : le s. 2 est clairement *29*, alors que dans le dernier mot du texte apparaît un exemple de *30*, ce qui peut faire penser, soit à l'existence de deux signes franchement différents, soit à une variation du dessin à l'intérieur d'un même texte, § 6. Comme argument pour la seconde explication, il faut signaler ici la ressemblance[2] avec le second mot d'une stèle de Saqqâra déjà connue, 47 bis F = **B** M–Y, soit *u-30-s-n-u*.

Le dernier mot est également remarquable : c'est apparemment une forme 'longue', en face de la forme 'courte' *d-30-o-v-25* qui est le second mot de la stèle déjà citée ; les ressemblances entre les deux stèles sont donc frappantes.[3] Mais il demeure une difficulté pour la forme 'longue' supposée : on attend la finale courante *25-h-e*, alors que la lecture du signe *38* est évidente. La présence ici d'une séquence *h-38* parallèle à *h-e* serait alors en faveur d'une valeur vocalique de ce signe, § 8.

29. H5–1435. Musée du Caire, JdE 91375   Plate XVII, 2

Hauteur 30 cm. ; largeur 17.9 cm. ; épaisseur 5 cm.

Calcaire. Même provenance que **28**.

Stèle très endommagée dans la partie gauche ; une partie indéterminée de l'inscription a disparu, dont il ne subsiste que des éléments horizontaux sur l'encadrement extérieur et l'encadrement intérieur, de droite à gauche.

Première reproduction chez Emery, *JEA* 56 (1970), pl. XV, 3 (petite photographie inversée au tirage) ; d'où Zauzich, p. 22, *Q* (dans le bon sens).

Belle gravure, signes réguliers et assez profonds.

(1) *th-d-a-7-e-25* | --- (2) *14-29* (ou *30*)*-v-a-44-e-25*

L. 1. Le premier mot est isolé. La dimension de ce qui suivait ne peut être déterminée, car le texte pouvait descendre sur le montant gauche.

L. 2. D'après la structure, il paraît s'agir d'un mot complet. Pour le s. 2, on peut hésiter entre *29* et *30*. Le s. 5, tracé avec netteté, est nouveau et particulier à Saqqâra ; serait-ce une forme 'renversée' de *43* ? Voir § 8.[4]

[1] *RHA* 1964, p. 27 et 40 ; *Issledovanija*, p. 309, 336 (index), etc.

[2] Je remercie M. Meier, qui a attiré mon attention sur ce point.

[3] Une autre observation peut être faite. Sur la stèle antérieurement connue, l'ordre des mots ne prête à aucune hésitation : *u-30-s-n-u* | *d-30-o-v-25 n-v-s-e-25*. Or, si l'on suppose que, sur la nouvelle stèle, ce que nous avons considéré comme le premier mot serait en réalité le troisième

(gravé en dernier lieu, sur le côté droit), on obtiendrait l'ordre suivant : *32-29-s-n-u-25* [...] *d-30-o-v-25-h-38 th-a-v-m-s-e-25*, avec une structure encore plus comparable.

[4] La comparaison suggérée par Zauzich, loc. cit., avec le s. 15 d'une autre stèle, 43 F = **G** M–Y, est tout à fait spécieuse, car il doit s'agir là d'une graphie maladroite de ▽ ou *29*, avec les hastes verticales écartées ; ce signe est d'ailleurs fréquent à l'initiale.

30. H5–1440. A Oxford, Ashmolean Museum, 1971.107 Plate XVIII, 1

Hauteur actuelle 34 cm.; largeur 24.5 cm.; épaisseur 6 cm.
Calcaire. Même provenance que **28**.
Stèle très endommagée et reconstituée en partie. Le texte, disposé sur l'encadrement extérieur, est à peu près intact. Orientation en deux sens.

□ Ӎ Ѵ Ι Φ Υ Ꝑ Ꝓ Ρ

Α Ϝ Ꝋ ⠂⠄ Ⓘ Χ Ꝋ Ο □ Ϲ

Gravure assez irégulière, avec de grandes hastes. Pour la disposition, il faut reconnaître une double orientation: (1) la partie horizontale est clairement sinistroverse; (2) la partie verticale, à gauche, est dextroverse, avec début en haut à gauche; les signes F et C sont d'ailleurs orientés à droite. Comparer **28**, avec une combinaison différente.

(1) *r-28-e-k-25 | u-m-27* (2) *a-v-e-?-25-h-e-o-27-g*

Le premier mot[1] est isolé à Saqqâra. Cependant, il convient d'en rapprocher le quatrième mot du graffite de Gebel Sheikh Suleiman, 72 F,[2] qui est probablement à lire *r-28-r-k-25*, la barre médiane chez Sayce devant être fortuite; en outre, si le second *r* a été mal lu, au lieu d'un *e*, on aurait exactement le même mot; pour une autre ressemblance avec Saqqâra, voir **22**. Ensuite, la formule postposée *u-m-27*, § 12, 2.

Le dernier mot, à en juger par l'absence de séparation, semble long, avec dix signes. Toutefois, la présence vers la fin de la séquence *25-h-e* inviterait à proposer une coupure; mais alors, que faire de *o-27-g*?[3]

31. H5–1501. British Museum, 67242 Plate XVIII, 2

Hauteur actuelle 25 cm.; largeur 20.3 cm.; épaisseur 6 cm.
Calcaire. Même provenance que **28**.
Stèle très endommagée: il ne subsiste qu'une partie de l'élément horizontal et un élément vertical, à gauche; orientation sinistroverse.

Ⓘ Ꝙ △ Ꝋ ✛ Ⴈ ⊿ Ι

Grandes lettres, peu régulières.

(1) ---(?)]-*n-k-o-25*-[(?) (2) ? | *a-v-h-e-d-a-25*

L. 1. Le mot subsistant est *n-k-o-25*, déjà bien connu, cf. **8**, etc.

---

[1] On notera la forme du signe *25*: avec l'élément vertical prolongé vers le bas, il ressemble à un *phi*. Ce ne peut être une attestation isolée de *20*, qui est propre à la Carie, mais occasionnellement, on a prolongé l'élément vertical de *25*, notamment à Abou-Simbel; voir § 8.

[2] Sur ce graffite, voir ci-dessus le commentaire de **22** et la note.

[3] Il pourrait s'agir d'une formule postposée de trois signes; l'absence de parallèle rend cette hypothèse fragile.

L. 2. Le mot subsistant a quelque ressemblance avec un mot de **14**, *a-v-14-a-é-25* ; le cinquième signe semble être un *d* tracé obliquement (comme les deux A du même mot).

32. H5–1506 + H6–374. A Durham, Gulbenkian Museum, 1971.140 + Saqqâra   Plate XIX, 1

Hauteur 30.2 cm.; largeur 20.4 cm.; épaisseur 6 cm.

Calcaire. Provenances: les trois quarts de la stèle viennent du même secteur que **28** etc., tandis que le coin inférieur droit (374) a été trouvé en 'H6', secteur 3 (campagne de 1968–1969).

Stèle endommagée et reconstituée. Elle est d'un type rudimentaire, avec un seul encadrement (comme **27**). Le texte est disposé de gauche à droite, horizontalement, puis à droite, verticalement (en colonne).

Assez bonne graphie; direction dextroverse évidente, avec F et N.

$$m\text{-}d\text{-}\d{t}h\text{-}o \mid m\text{-}e\text{-}d\text{-}v\text{-}n\text{-}25\text{-}h\text{-}e \mid n\text{-}32\text{-}g\text{-}o\text{-}k\text{-}25\text{-}h\text{-}e$$

Premier mot assez court; le s. 3 est très probablement un *th*. Second mot isolé.

Le troisième mot est le terme banal en position finale, § 12, 1. Noter la forme du signe *32*, qui semble fermé comme dans **6** ; hésitation entre ⊓ et ⊔ ?

33. H5–1507. Musée du Caire, JdE 91374   Plate XIX, 2

Hauteur 32.5 cm.; largeur 21.5 cm.; épaisseur 6.7 cm.

Même provenance que **28**, etc.

Belle stèle, dont la partie inscrite est intacte. Le texte est disposé de gauche à droite, sur l'encadrement intérieur, à partir du milieu à gauche.

Gravure assez régulière, direction dextroverse évidente. En dépit du bon état de la pierre et du soin apparent avec lequel elle a été gravée, l'inscription pose un problème pour son début. En effet, au milieu, à gauche, on voit une petite barre, puis les lettres *o-v-25*, qui ressemblent à une fin de mot, et non pas à un vocable complet; on a d'ailleurs ensuite la formule *32-m-27*. Il semble donc que, pour des raisons obscures, le lapicide n'ait jamais gravé le début du premier mot.

$$\mid (?)\ o\text{-}v\text{-}25 \mid 32\text{-}m\text{-}27 \mid th\text{-}g\text{-}a\text{-}v\text{-}42\text{-}o\text{-}u\text{-}25 \mid 14\text{-}42\text{-}h\text{-}a\text{-}14\text{-}a\text{-}v\text{-}25$$

Pour le début du texte, voir ci-dessus; la finale *o-v-25* connue par *d-30-o-v-25*, sur **47 bis** F = *B* M–Y, voir le commentaire de **28**.[1] La formule postposée *32-m-27* figure déjà sur **28**, voir § 12, 2.

La troisième séquence est isolée; elle contient le signe rare *42*, comme la stèle **26**. La quatrième séquence, qui renferme aussi le signe *42*, se trouve, en même position, sur **26**.

[1] On a plusieurs finales en 'voyelle + *v-25*', argument supplémentaire pour voir ici un mot inachevé.

34. H5–1832. Musée du Caire, JdE 91516   Plates XX, 1; XXXVI, 4

Hauteur 33.5 cm.; largeur 23.5 cm.; épaisseur 6.5 cm.

Calcaire. Provenance: secteur 3, à l'ouest du 'South Screen Wall', dans la cour de ce qui a été appelé 'tombe carienne', sous des cabanes d'ouvriers.[1] Campagne 1969–1970.

Belle stèle intacte. Le texte est disposé sur les encadrements extérieur et intérieur, de droite à gauche; début à droite, au milieu.

ΘΧ:ΦϘΑΜΠΝ:⬜Υ:ΦΝΟΗＦΑ

ΘΧ:Φ↑ϽΘＦ↑Ϙ ΘΧ:ΦΥΟϽΠΝ

L'inscription est gravée et disposée avec le plus grand soin; les séparations, nombreuses, sont marquées par deux ou trois points superposés. La direction sinistroverse est évidente.

    (1) *a-v-38-o-n-25 : u-27 : n-32-s-a-14-25 : h-e : n-32-g-o-k-25 : h-e*
    (2) *14-l-v-e-g-l-31-25 : h-e*

Pour la structure des mots cariens, cette stèle est précieuse, et présente un caractère unique. En effet, chacune des séquences longues est suivie de deux signes, qui sont soigneusement séparés de ce qui précède par la marque de séparation. Cette délimitation, qui n'est pas due au hasard, prouve que les éléments de deux signes sont séparables et peuvent représenter des formules postposées; on l'avait déjà soupçonné pour l'élément *h-e*, § 12, 3, et ceci est devenu clair, également, pour *u-27*, disposé de la même manière sur **20** (voir aussi **43**), qui est une formule du même type que *u-m-27*, § 12, 2.

Les séquences longues sont isolées,[2] sauf la troisième qui est le mot fréquent à Saqqâra, § 12, 1, ici en position pénultième.

35. H5–1833. Musée du Caire, JdE 91515   Plate XX, 2

Hauteur 37.5 cm.; largeur 19.3 cm.; épaisseur 6 cm.

Calcaire. Même provenance que **34**.

Belle stèle intacte. Le texte est disposé symétriquement sur l'encadrement extérieur, de droite à gauche; début en bas à droite.

Ϙ△ΙΘ+ΦΟΥΝΙΦΝΟΘ△ＦΑ

ΙꝹΧΦ⊕Υ⊕ＰΑΙ⬜ΜＶΙΦΘΜΧ

Φ↑△ΟΜꝹ

[1] Note de G. T. Martin à ce sujet: 'There does not appear to be any evidence for calling the structure a tomb; it appears to have been a house of some kind, in which stelae were found. But more research will have to be done on this point.'

[2] Les quatre derniers signes du premier mot se retrouvent cependant dans **4**, quatrième mot, et **24**, second mot (remarque de M. Meier).

Gravure régulière; texte long, avec six mots bien séparés.

a-v-d-e-o-n-25 | *n-k-o-25-h-e* | *d-28-h-s-e-25* | *u-m-27* | *a-v-th-u-th-25-h-e* | *29-s-o-d-l-25*

Le premier mot, en *a-v-d-e*, ressemble au mot initial de **1** et **7** et, d'une autre manière, au mot initial de **34**, *a-v-38-o-n-25*. Le second mot est la variante en *h-e* de *n-k-o-25*, fourni par **8**, etc. Le troisième mot est isolé, mais pourvu de la formule postposée *u-m-27*, § 12, 2.

Le quatrième mot *a-v-th-u-th-25-h-e* représente une forme 'longue' en *h-e* par rapport à la forme 'courte' qui figure dans **36**. Ces deux termes sont à comparer avec *th-u-th-25*, en **9**. On doit alors se demander si *a-v* serait ici un élément séparable;[1] de toute manière, un certain nombre de mots comportent un début en *a-v*; voir les index A et B.

Le dernier mot est isolé.

36. H5–1872. Musée du Caire, JdE 91517   Plates XXI, 1; XXXVII, 1

Hauteur 26.3 cm.; largeur 19.1 cm.; épaisseur 8 cm.
Calcaire. Même provenance que **34**.
Stèle presque carrée. Texte disposé sur la corniche et sur l'encadrement extérieur, de droite à gauche; début en bas à droite.

Gravure assez négligée, mais nette; pas de marques de séparation. La disposition du premier mot sur la corniche, est remarquable: la 'désinence' *h-e* a été rajoutée en lettres plus petites, à gauche; cf. § 12, 3.

(1) *n-32-14-o-k-25-h-e*   (2) *a-m-n-27-k*   *a̦-v-th-u-th-25*   *30-o-38-o-7-h-e*

L. 1. Le premier mot est une variante de *n-32-g-o-k-25-h-e*, ordinairement en position finale, avec comme troisième lettre le signe *14* au lieu du C ou *g* courant ailleurs, § 8.[2]

L. 2. Le second mot, finale en *27-k*, est isolé. Il se termine certainement en haut de l'encadrement, car le mot suivant, placé horizontalement, correspond au cinquième mot de **35**, moins l'élément *h-e*.

Le quatrième mot est isolé.

37. H5–1873. A Londres, University College, 2406   Plate XXI, 2

Hauteur 28.5 cm.; largeur 19.5 cm.; épaisseur 6.7 cm.
Calcaire. Même provenance que **34**.

---

[1] De son côté, V. Ševoroškin, *Issledovanija*, p. 323, a cru pouvoir dégager un élément radical *av-*, en proposant divers 'découpages' de mots cariens.
[2] Voir *Kadmos* 16 (1977), p. 92.

Belle stèle, endommagée en haut; disposition entièrement horizontale, de gauche à droite, deux lignes sur la corniche, la troisième sur l'encadrement supérieur. Au-dessus de la 'porte', ornement en bouton de lotus (cf. **15**).

Gravure fine et régulière, dextroverse; le début des ll. 1–2 est endommagé.

(1) *?-?-d-a-7-e-s*   (2) *?-e-a-n-25-h-e*   (3) *a-d-o-s-h-a-v-k-o-s*

Le premier mot est isolé et ne peut être restitué; noter la finale rare en *e-s*, cf. **27**. Même remarque pour le début du second mot.

Le troisième mot est intact et long, mais isolé; noter la finale en *-o-s*.

38. H5–1980. A Londres, University College, 2403   Plate XXII, 1, 2

Hauteur 38.5 cm.; largeur 25 cm.
Calcaire. Même provenance que **34**.
Cette stèle porte une inscription gravée superficiellement et de manière négligée, ce qui est rare à Saqqâra. Disposition horizontale, sur la corniche et sur l'encadrement supérieur, de droite à gauche.

Du fait de sa mauvaise gravure, l'inscription est difficile à lire, surtout à la fin de la l. 2, avec des lettres plus petites, et un retour à droite.

(1) *n-32-g-o-k-25-h-e*   (2) *28-a-s-31-25 | é-e-25-h-l-e-29-s-h-e-25*

L. 1. Pour le premier mot, voir **36**, avec l'orthographe normale ici.

L. 2. Le second mot est isolé.

L. 3. Le dernier mot, particulièrement long, est isolé; le début en *é-e* est fourni par **17**, *é-e-a-s-e-...*

IV. Objets divers et fragments

39. H5–1346. British Museum, 67255   Plates XXIII, 1; XXXVII, 2

Plaque de calcaire, 26×48 cm., épaisseur 5.5 cm.
Même provenance que **1**.
Cette plaque est décorée sur la surface de motifs floraux tracés à la peinture, en couleur brun-violet, avec quatorze rangées de sept motifs. La destination de cet objet n'apparaît pas.[1] Sur une des quatre faces latérales,

[1] Je n'ai pas pu trouver d'élément de comparaison pour cette pièce.

dans un cadre rectangulaire incisé de façon régulière, inscription carienne de dix-neuf signes, sinistroverse, mais disposée dans le sens inverse par rapport à la surface décorée. On a probablement affaire à un remploi.

L'inscription est très soigneusement gravée; du fait d'une détérioration à gauche, il manque probablement deux signes.

14-30-14-27-s | m-a-v-a-e-43-v-27-7-25-h-e | n-k-[--

Le premier mot est isolé; début probable en *14-30* dans **29,** dernier mot; il se termine en *-s.*

Le second mot est très long, avec douze signes, et contient, en sixième place, le signe rare *43*; voir § 8. Le début en *m-a-v-a-* est déjà attesté sur l'Apis de bronze, 45 F = **K** M–Y, (1) *m-a-v-a-27-é-n*; voir aussi les remarques sur **17,** deuxième mot, début en *m-a-v* et fin en *n-25-h-e.*

Le dernier mot, en *n-k,* devait être court; il y a peut-être la place pour *n-k-[o-25],* cf. **8, 19,** etc.

40. H6–418. A Londres, University College, 2404   Plates XXIII, 2; XXXVII, 3

Bloc de calcaire presque carré, brisé en bas; hauteur à gauche 16 cm., à droite 19 cm.; largeur en haut 16 cm., en bas 17 cm.; épaisseur 7.5 cm.

Provenance: 'surface débris, Sector 3'; 1968.

Cette pierre constitue probablement la partie supérieure d'une stèle rectangulaire assez grossière.[1] En haut, un espace vide; en dessous, restes de quatre lignes horizontales, à lire de droite à gauche.

Inscription curieusement disposée et incisée. Les lettres ont été soigneusement disposées en colonnes, comme dans un texte *stoichédon,* et d'abord tracées en pointillé dans la pierre; ensuite, plusieurs signes ont été complétés par des incisions entre les points, mais ce travail n'a pas été achevé par le lapicide. La lecture sinistroverse est assurée: *vacat* en bas à gauche, orientation de F et C, structure générale.

     (1) *?-?-38-?-25*   (2) *?-o-32-14-25*   (3) *h-e : n-s-k*   (4) *o-v-ẹ-25*

L. 1–3. Le début est effacé; on a deux mots, ou plutôt un mot long de douze lettres, finale en *25-h-e*; comparer alors le second mot de **5.**

L. 3–4. Une séparation par : est bien visible après *h-e.* Ensuite un mot commençant par *n-s-k-o,* ce qui confirme le découpage des mots sur la stèle de Bruxelles, 48 F = **D** M–Y, dernier mot

---

[1] 'I feel sure that it was originally a stela (but not a false-door type), which was broken for re-use as masonry, doubtless for the blocking of a niche in the Baboon galleries. The top and both sides look as if they have been "trimmed" for re-use; the chisel-marks are present, the sides are not smooth. There are traces of plaster on the left side; the bottom has been broken off' (note par G. T. Martin).

n-s-k-o-v-e-25; en définitive, on a la même séquence à finale *o-v-e-25* sur cette stèle et ici. Pour la finale, comparer **21**, second mot en *n-o-v-e-25*.

41. H5–1565. A Saqqâra, dépôt des antiquités — Plate XXIII, 3

Bloc de calcaire, hauteur 26 à 27 cm., largeur 42 cm., épaisseur 27 cm.
Provenance: 'found in the débris of the Baboon Gallery...'.
Cette pierre, remployée dans le souterrain, pourrait être une stèle de forme oblongue.[1] Elle porte une inscription de gravure assez irrégulière, signes de 11 à 50 mm. La direction de l'écriture paraît être d'abord dextroverse, ensuite sinistroverse.

(1) *d-o-u-l-a-32* | *s-e*   (2) *v-a-d* | *m-k-d-31-25-32-d*

Le principal problème posé par ce texte est la direction des lignes. Une tentative de lecture entièrement sinistroverse ne donne pas un bon résultat pour la l. 1.[2] Il est donc probable qu'on a affaire à texte *boustrophédon*,[3] d'abord dextroverse, puis sinistroverse. A la l. 1, le s. 4, un *l* dextroverse, et à la l. 2, le s. 1, un F sinistroverse, sont en faveur d'une telle disposition. En outre, la structure générale du texte et celle des deux premiers mots se présentent dans de bien meilleures conditions.

Le premier mot, en *d-o-u-l*, fait penser à *d-e-u-l-*... sur une stèle du Louvre, 47 F = A M–Y;[4] le s. 5 me paraît incertain, un *a* irrégulier plutôt qu'un *d* ? Le second mot, *s-e-v-a-d*, possède une finale en *a-d* qui est connue en Égypte; voir les index A et B, index inverse. En outre, avec une variation du vocalisme, on peut le rapprocher du terme *s-a-v-a* qui figure à la fin de la stèle de Lausanne, 46 F, ici Appendice II. Quant au dernier mot, avec un début en *m-k-d*, plutôt que *m-k-a*, il est isolé.

42. 'Inscr. 10', Saqqâra, *in situ*, 'lower Baboon Gallery' — Plate XXXVII, 4

Cette pierre, demeurée dans un mur du souterrain,[5] est très probablement, comme la précédente, une stèle de forme oblongue, remployée; il ne s'agit donc pas, comme on l'avait envisagé initialement, d'un graffite incisé par un Carien de passage dans cette galerie.[6] Deux lignes, sinistroverses.
Dimensions: d'après le fac-similé, ligne 1, 9.5 cm.; ligne 2, 13.5 cm.

[1] 'Probably a reused block, used for sealing the wall of a Baboon niche' (G. T. Martin, 1973).

[2] Ainsi que me l'a fait observer M. Meier.

[3] Cette disposition est intéressante; pour une double orientation, comparer **28** et **30**.

[4] Noter aussi l'existence d'une séquence *d-o-u* à Abou-Simbel, 72 Š, premier mot *m-a-v-25-o-d-o-u*.

[5] La position précise est: 'Built into bottom of North Wall (22 niches West of 8, 9).' En raison de la position de la pierre, il n'a pas été possible de la photographier; restée en place, elle n'a pas reçu de numéro dans la série 'H5'.

[6] Cette hypothèse avait été envisagée par W. B. Emery, *JEA* 56 (1970), p. 8: 'However, we must note that among the numerous graffiti on the walls of the galleries is one in Carian, which suggests the galleries were in existence at the time when the stelae were in use.' Cette interprétation est impossible: 'the stone on which the inscription is cut was certainly reused, presumably with the Carian inscription already on it' (G. T. Martin, 1973).

La gravure est assez régulière, et l'ensemble d'une facture très supérieure à celle de la pierre précédente.

ϙⱶᴠᴠ□þ

þ+Ⲫϙ∨ꝑℳ+ɯ

(1) *r-27-k-u-v-14*   (2) *m-h-s-e-n-14-25-h-e*

L. 1. Début en *r-27*, sans parallèle.
L. 2. Début rare en *m-h-s-e*, comparer *m-s-e* en **43**?

43. H5–1819. A Londres, British Museum, 67241   Plates XXIV, 1; XXXVII, 5

Pierre de forme semi-circulaire, largeur 25 cm.
Calcaire. Provenance: 'Débris in Sector 3, west of the "South Screen Wall".'

Il doit s'agir de la partie supérieure d'une stèle cintrée, sans décoration ni rebord incisé; comparer ici **9** et **11**, ainsi que la stèle de Grenoble, 74 F = **C** M–Y (largeur 25 cm.) ou celle de Bruxelles, 48 F = **D** M–Y (largeur 29.5 cm.). L'inscription est gravée en suivant le rebord supérieur (ce qui rappelle la disposition de la stèle de Bruxelles).

Ψ◊ⱶ▽ꝑℳℳI Ⲫþꝑ△ⱵA

□ᴠ

Les signes sont gravés finement, mais avec soin: une ligne sous le rebord, plus deux signes à droite, à peu près sous le début, gravure de droite à gauche.

(1) *a-v-d-e-r-25 | m-s-e-29-v-o-ḳ-*[?   (2) *u-27*

L. 1. Le premier mot est déjà connu, même position initiale, sur **1** et **7**. Le second mot a un début en *m-s*, mais pour le reste, il paraît isolé. La finale est difficile: d'une part, il est impossible de savoir si le texte se poursuivait après le s. 13; d'autre part, ce signe est endommagé; plutôt que *25*, qui serait peut-être suggéré par la photographie, on voit sur la pierre les traces d'un *k*.[1]

L. 2. La petite séquence *u-27* doit se rattacher à la fin du texte, et se trouve placée à part, comme formule postposée, voir § 12, 2; si l'inscription est complète, on aurait un mot terminé par *o-ḳ-u-27*.

44. H5–1504. A Londres, British Museum, 67248   Plate XXIV, 2

Fragment (partie supérieure) de stèle fausse-porte, hauteur 10.4 cm.; largeur 18 cm.
Calcaire. Même provenance que **28**, etc.

Il ne subsiste qu'une partie impossible à déterminer du texte, surtout l'élément horizontal, sur le rebord extérieur; mais le texte commençait évidemment à droite et se poursuivait à gauche.

⟩ⴸIⲪ◊ⱶℲⱶ⟩Ⱶⱸ

---

[1] Il serait plus normal d'avoir ici *25* et en conséquence, un mot complet à finale en | *u-27*, comparer **20**, ... *-25* | *u-27* et **34**, ... *-25*: *u-27*, mais je ne veux pas 'corriger' le lapicide.

Assez bonne gravure, sinistroverse.

$$\text{---]-}a\text{-}v\text{-}g\text{-}é\text{-}l\text{-}é\text{-}v\text{-}25 \mid n\text{-}g\text{-}[\text{----}$$

Ce fragment n'est pas dépourvu d'intérêt. Dans la première séquence conservée, on note la présence de deux exemplaires très clairs du signe *5* ou *é*, en forme d'epsilon à trois branches, avec la haste verticale prolongée vers le bas. D'autre part, il n'est nullement certain que le *a* représente le début du mot (un trait oblique placé juste avant est ambigu : barre de séparation ou partie gauche d'un signe ?). Si c'était le cas, le mot obtenu aurait une certaine ressemblance avec la légende d'une monnaie carienne de Carie (site d'émission non connu), qui se lit *a-40-g-v-l-e-25* ; naturellement, ce rapprochement n'est que partiel, et je ne peux expliquer les divergences, mais il mérite sans doute d'être signalé, de même que tout autre élément susceptible de réunir les documents d'Égypte et de Carie.[1]

De la deuxième séquence, il ne subsiste que le début, *n-g-[* ; on a des mots commençant par *n-g-a* dans **3**, **9**, **10** et **25**.

45. H5–353. A Cambridge, Fitzwilliam Museum, E.10.1969   Plate XXIV, 3

Fragment de corniche, venant d'une stèle fausse-porte, largeur 14.4 cm., hauteur 9.4 cm. Calcaire. 'Found in surface débris, Square H5.'

Sur ce fragment, cinq signes correspondant à la fin d'une inscription ; traces de couleur rouge et bleue dans les lettres.

$$\text{---]-}th\text{-}25\text{-}s\text{-}e\text{-}25$$

Finale en *e-25*.

45a. H6–372. A Londres, British Museum, 67246   Plate XXV, 1

Fragment venant d'une stèle fausse-porte, largeur 14 cm., hauteur 7.5 à 10 cm. Calcaire. 'Surface débris, Sector 3.'

Gravure irrégulière.

$$n\text{-}\underset{.}{v}\text{-}s\text{-}\underset{.}{38}\text{-}[$$

Malgré l'aspect irrégulier des deux premières lettres, l'interprétation est assurée ; en effet, on peut comparer un mot de même structure, *n-v-s-e-25*, voir **18** et le commentaire.

46. H6–373. British Museum, 67245   Plate XXV, 2

Fragment de nature indéterminée, largeur 12.4 cm., hauteur max. 4.2 cm. Calcaire. Même provenance que **45a**.

Quatre signes, début d'un mot.

$$m\text{-}s\text{-}n\text{-}a\text{-}[\text{---}$$

Ce début de mot, malheureusement mutilé, est intéressant car il confirme l'existence à Saqqâra

---

[1] J'ai déjà signalé ce fait, en republiant la monnaie carienne, dans *Kadmos* 13 (1974), p. 126.

du radical *m(e)sn-*, déjà fourni par la stèle de Lausanne, 46 F = **F** M–Y (plus loin, Appendice II); voir le commentaire de **50,** ligne 2.

47. H5–1505. British Museum, 67247 Plate XXV, 3

Fragment de stèle fausse-porte, partie inférieure droite; largeur 16.4 cm., hauteur 13 cm. Calcaire. Même provenance que **28,** etc.

Début d'inscription, en bas à droite.

e-a-v-29-[--

Début d'un mot, en *e-a,* d'un type rare; pas d'autre exemple en Égypte.

47a. H5–1503. British Museum, 67250 Plate XXVI, 1

Fragment de stèle fausse-porte, partie inférieure gauche; hauteur 15.2 cm., largeur 7.5 cm. Calcaire. 'Found in the débris, N.W. corner of Sector 3.'

Fin d'une inscription, avec quatre signes.

---]-e-25-h-e

Finale de type banal.

47b. H6–386. British Museum, 67240 Plate XXVI, 2

Fragment de nature indéterminée, largeur 10.5 cm., hauteur 11 cm. Calcaire. 'Found in surface débris, east side of Sector 3.'

--]-s-25-ḥ-e

Finale de type banal.

48. H5–2432. British Museum, 67244 Plate XXVI, 3

Petit fragment de stèle fausse-porte, coin supérieur gauche, hauteur 5.6 cm., largeur 4.2 cm. Calcaire. 'Surface débris, Square H5.'

--]-u-14-v-[--

48a. H5–35. A Saqqâra, dépôt des antiquités Plate XXVI, 4

Fragment de stèle fausse-porte, rebord, largeur 6.5 cm. Calcaire. 'Surface débris, Square H5.'

--]?-h-25

48b. S 72/3–42. A Saqqâra, même dépôt que **48a**

Fragment, largeur 5.3 cm., hauteur 2.7 cm. Calcaire. 'Sector 7, surface débris.'

--]-?-e

48c. S 72/3–39. Même situation que **48a**

Fragment, largeur 4 cm., hauteur 4.5 cm.
Calcaire. Même provenance que **48b**.

--]-?-25-[--

48d. S 74/5–20. Même situation que **48a**   Plate XXVI, 3

Fragment de stèle fausse-porte, partie supérieure, largeur 18.6 cm., hauteur maximum 16.2 cm.
Calcaire. 'Found in a robbers' pit 5 m. west of the gate of the Baboon Dromos, 1.60 m. below pavement level.'

Dans un espace ménagé intentionnellement, six lettres gravées avec peu de soin; en dessous, une lettre N.

e-g-é-27-s-25

Le mot semble complet, avec le dernier signe plus bas à gauche. Pour un début en *e-g*, voir **10** et **25**, mais la suite diffère.

49. S 75/6–24. Même situation que **48a**

Fragment de stèle cintrée, partie supérieure gauche, hauteur 10 cm., larg. maximum 11 cm., épaisseur 5 cm.
'Found reused in the paving of the north–south Sacred Way across the temple precinct.'

Sous un lignage horizontal, restes de trois fins de lignes.

(1) ----]-ṣ-27 : m-g   (2) ----]-?-n-e   (3) ---

Texte trop détérioré. L. 1, au lieu de -ṣ-27, peut-être une finale en *ṃ-27*. Ensuite, début d'un mot en *m-g*, comme dans **51**, 3, et ailleurs.[1]

---

[1] Il paraît inutile de cataloguer et de décrire en détail un autre fragment de stèle fausse-porte, S 75/6–28 (6392), avec des restes misérables, dont le signe *25*.

B. INSCRIPTIONS CARIENNES DE BOUHEN

DURANT la campagne exécutée à Bouhen[1] en 1962–1963, sous la direction de W. B. Emery, pour le compte de l'Egypt Exploration Society, les archéologues britanniques ont dégagé le temple du sud ou temple d'Hatshepsout,[2] afin de démonter ses éléments et de les faire transporter à Khartoum; c'est près du nouveau musée de cette ville que le temple a été reconstitué.

Au cours de ces travaux,[3] une importante inscription carienne, jusqu'ici inconnue, a été dégagée;[4] d'autres, qui avaient été copiées jadis par A. H. Sayce, ont été retrouvées à cette occasion. Il a donc paru opportun de faire suivre la publication du nouveau document par une réédition des autres graffites, en donnant ici un *corpusculum* des inscriptions de Bouhen.[5]

50. Inv. 1616 (K. 11.4). A Khartoum, nouveau musée (?)   Plates XXVII, 1; XXXVIII,1

Bloc, largeur 64.5 cm.; hauteur 39 cm.; épaisseur 15 cm.
Provenance: 'Block of sandstone found reused in the right jamb of the late gateway giving access from the South to the entrance of the South temple...'.[6]
Graffite sur cinq lignes occupant presque toute la surface du bloc, de droite à gauche.

---

[1] Le site de Bouhen, aujourd'hui disparu sous les eaux, se trouvait sur la rive ouest du Nil, opposé à la bourgade moderne de Ouadi Halfa; il ne convient pas d'attribuer les inscriptions à 'Wadi Halfa' même, comme le faisait Friedrich, 66–71 F.

[2] Ce temple a été longtemps dénommé 'temple de Thoutmosis III'; voir Porter–Moss, *Topographical Bibliography*, vii (1951), p. 131 sqq. Il est maintenant décrit comme 'The Southern Temple' par R. A. Caminos, *The New-Kingdom Temples of Buhen*, i, Londres, 1974; ouvrage cité plus loin comme *Buhen*, i.

[3] Résumés chez J. Leclant, *Orientalia* 33 (1964), p. 375–377; 34 (1965), p. 211–212. Rapport préliminaire de W. B. Emery, *Kush* 12 (1964), p. 43–46.

[4] Découverte signalée par O. Masson, *Bull. Soc. Fr. Égyptologie* 56, novembre 1969, p. 31; *Kadmos* 8 1969), p. 170; J. Leclant, *Orientalia* 40 (1971), p. 248.

[5] Les graffites grecs qui ont été découverts par l'expédition britannique sont publiés par O. Masson, *Chronique d'Égypte* 51 (1976), p. 310–313.

[6] 'It showed on discovery traces of painted plaster adhering, perhaps part of a Nubian Christian fresco; on their removal, five lines of incised Carian inscription were discovered... It seems probable that this block, like others, bearing Greek and Carian mercenaries' inscriptions and subsequently built into brick reconstructions, may originally have formed part of Taharka's screen wall, though it bears no surviving inscriptions' (indications communiquées par H. S. Smith).

Très soigneusement incisé, avec une marge régulière à droite et assez régulière à gauche, des signes de belle facture, ce texte ressemble davantage à une véritable inscription qu'à un graffite; cependant, il a dû être gravé sur une paroi du temple, avant le remploi du bloc. Le texte est complet, sauf dans le coin supérieur droit, où le début des l. 1–2 a disparu.

(1) *?-?-n-s-a-d* | *a-v*   (2) [*d*]-*e-r* | *m-s-n-a-25*   (3) *u-25* | *u-v-n-25* | *a-k*
(4) *29-43-u-r* | *40-v-27-d*   (5) *29-31-o-u-25*

L. 1. Au début du premier mot, lacune de deux signes. Il se termine en *s-a-d*, de même que le premier mot de **51**, mais le début ne concorde pas.

Le second mot, à cheval sur deux lignes, est facile à restituer, avec un [*d*] dans la lacune; en effet, il est clair maintenant que le même mot reparaît comme second mot dans **51**, *a-v-ḍ-e-r*; d'autre part, la forme plus longue, *a-v-d-e-r-25*, est connue dorénavant à Saqqâra, **1**, **7** et **43**. Enfin, un petit graffite d'Abydos, **18 F**, longtemps lu *a-v-a-e-25*, est clairement *a-v-d-e-r*, selon la révision de J. Yoyotte.

L. 2. On a ici le début du second mot, formé sur le radical *m-s-n-a* qui est bien connu en carien d'Égypte. A Bouhen même, il existe deux exemples de *m-s-n-a-25-n*, **53** et **54**; à Thèbes, **57 Š**, et à Silsile, **53 F**, on trouve *m-s-n-a-25*. Il faut évidemment rapprocher *m-e-s-n-a-* à Abou-Simbel, avec **78 Š**, finale *a-25-30*, et **74 Š**, finale *a-r-29*. A Saqqâra même, il y a d'une part la forme incomplète *m-s-n-a*[, **46**, et d'autre part, sur la stèle de Lausanne, **46 F** = **F M–Y**, le premier mot qui est à lire désormais *m-s-n-r-29*; voir plus loin, Appendice II. Dans la présente inscription, il semble donc qu'on a *m-s-n-a-25* élargi par *u-25*.

L. 3. Le mot du milieu, ou quatrième mot, *u-v-n-25*, est à comparer avec *u-v-o-n-25* dans **51**, mais ces formes ne reviennent pas ailleurs.

L. 4. A cheval sur la ligne précédente et celle-ci, le mot *a-k-29-43-u-r* est notable. Il comporte en quatrième position le signe rare *43*, maintenant connu à Saqqâra, voir §§ 6, 8. Or, le dernier mot du graffite **51** correspond lettre pour lettre à cette séquence, avec une seule difficulté en quatrième position: on voit confusément un demi-cercle, et deux petits traits à l'intérieur, ce qui faisait croire à la présence d'un F. Par la comparaison avec le nouveau texte, je crois qu'il faut lire désormais *43-u-r*. Mais ce mot est tout à fait isolé.

L. 4–5. La fin du texte est difficile à découper en mots: on pourrait voir, soit deux mots, soit un mot long de neuf signes. Dans la première hypothèse, on aurait d'abord un mot à finale *d*, soit *40-v-27-d*; noter à l'initiale la présence de la 'flèche' ou *40*, signe non encore connu à Bouhen.[1] Le dernier mot serait *29-31-o-u-25*.

51. Graffite 66 F. A Khartoum, dans le temple reconstruit   Plates XXVII, 2; XXXVIII, 2

Dimensions de la surface inscrite: larg. 42 cm., h. 36 cm. env.

Sur un panneau du pilastre 18, face nord; dans le coin inférieur gauche, sur les jambes de la déesse, cinq lignes incisées, de droite à gauche.

Ce graffite, très visible, a été copié deux fois par Sayce (d'où Friedrich, p. 105, fig. 66 et 66'), et vu ultérieurement par d'autres visiteurs. Il a été copié, dessiné et photographié à l'occasion des travaux de R. A. Caminos, grâce à qui une nouvelle édition peut être donnée ici.[2] Le texte, incisé

---

[1] Il est très rare en position initiale: deux exemples sur la stèle 48bis F = **H M–Y**.

[2] Voir Caminos, *Buhen*, i, p. 53–55, description du pilastre 18; pl. 64, 2 (vue générale); pl. 65, 1 (dessin) et 2 (photo Bellens et Vermeir).

sur un relief égyptien, demeure difficile en plusieurs endroits; on est aidé par les différentes copies, mais surtout par le nouveau graffite, **50**, dont la parenté avec **51** est frappante.

(1) *27-u-n-a-l-k-a*   (2) *s-a-d | a-v-ḍ-e-r*   (3) *m-g-14-o-n-25*   (4) *u-v-o-n-25 | a-ḳ*
(5) *29-43-u-r*

ΑΨΛΑΝV口

)ΘϽϝΑΙΔΑΜ

ΦΛΟႷ)ᏣᏣ

ΨϤΙΦΛΟϝΥ

ϷVϿϤ

L. 1. Au début, il semble bien qu'on ait un seul mot, long de dix signes, se terminant en *s-a-d* à la ligne 2; en effet, **50** commence par un mot beaucoup plus court, mais pareillement en *s-a-d*. Le dessin de Sayce est pratiquement confirmé: le s. 4 est un *a* de forme proche de celle du delta; le s. 5 a la forme du lambda grec à branches égales (cf. à Saqqâra **16**); après le *a* final, un léger trait vertical est clairement fortuit (ainsi Sayce, première copie) et ne doit pas compter pour une barre de séparation (Sayce, seconde copie, d'où Friedrich, etc.).[1]

L. 2. Aidé par le second mot de **50** et par des formes parallèles, il semble qu'on puisse lire ici *a-v-ḍ-e-r*, le doute ne subsistant que pour la troisième lettre (malheureusement disparue sur **50**!). Les autres lettres sont assurées et sont pratiquement données par la première copie de Sayce (la seconde est aberrante). Pour le s. 3, on peut supposer un *d* à la fois maladroit (arrondi ?) et endommagé par des traits fortuits; en tout cas, on doit comparer *a-v-d-e-r-25*, attesté à Saqqâra, **1, 7, 43**, ainsi que d'autres mots commençant par *a-v-d* (voir l'index).

L. 3. Un mot de six lettres, déjà bien copié par Sayce (première copie). Les lettres incertaines sont la seconde, en arc de cercle, probablement C tourné à gauche, et la quatrième, un *o* assez effacé; la finale *n-25* est claire.

L. 4. D'abord un mot *u-v-o-n-25*, dont toutes les lettres, bien vues par Sayce, sont assurées; ce mot rappelle de près *u-v-n-25* sur **50**, dans la même position, par rapport à la séquence suivante.

L. 5. Commençant à la ligne précédente, un mot de six lettres, qui correspond à un mot probablement identique de **50**, comme on l'a indiqué plus haut; le second signe de la ligne est difficile à établir, mais pourrait être le signe rare *43*, en partie défiguré.

En conclusion sur les graffites **50** et **51**, on doit remarquer qu'ils ont de nombreux points de contact, mais qu'il s'agit quand même de textes différents. Ils ont probablement été gravés au même moment, et peut-être par le même personnage.

[1] Dans *Issledovanija*, p. 316, fig. 80, Ševoroškin donne ce trait en pointillé. P. 335, index (avec d'autres références), il semble faire de *sad* un mot indépendant. A propos de cette finale, on pourrait peut-être comparer un mot à lire *th-32-s-a-ḍ* dans un graffite de Thèbes, 59 Š, en voyant à la fin un *d*, plutôt que *29* avec Ševoroškin.

52. Graffite 68 F   Plate XXVIII, 1

Longueur 23 cm. environ.

Sur un bloc autrefois détaché d'un montant et ultérieurement remis en place, 'incised along the right-hand margin of the south door-jamb (no. 20)'.[1] Sept ou huit signes, de droite à gauche.

$$\text{⁙ A Θ Þ A N Ọ}$$

Ce graffite, copié par Sayce en 1893–1894, a été retrouvé et copié par R. A. Caminos; les lettres sont assez effacées et il est difficile d'en déterminer le nombre exact.[2]

?-14-n-a-e-25-?-?

Une trace de signe devant *14*, qui est sûr. Les trois lettres suivantes sont reconnaissables; la suite est incertaine, peut-être *25-a-d* selon la copie de Sayce. L'ensemble est obscur.

53–54. Graffites 69 et 70 F

Dimensions inconnues.

Sur des blocs? Deux graffites connus seulement par les copies de Sayce et qui n'ont pas été retrouvés; on les reprend ici pour compléter l'ensemble. Orientation de droite à gauche.

$$\text{V: Φ A N M M}$$

$$\text{Φ Þ M ⅂ Ǝ Þ}$$

$$\text{V Φ A N M M}$$

53: (1) *m-s-n-a-25-ṇ*   (2) *e-ẹ́-v-s-e-25*
54: *m-s-n-a-25-n*

Les deux graffites, d'aspect comparable, sont peut-être l'œuvre du même personnage. La lecture est assurée, dans chacun, pour le mot *m-s-n-a-25-n*, voir **50**.[3] Le second mot du premier graffite est incertain pour la seconde lettre: un *é*? ou un *v* avec Bork-Friedrich?

55. Graffite 67 F. Au Musée des Antiquités de Khartoum, inv. 491   Plates XXVIII, 2; XXIX

Longueur 48 cm. environ, hauteur 27 cm. environ.

Graffite de trois lignes, incisé de droite à gauche sur la colonne 31, à gauche d'un texte hiéroglyphique disposé verticalement.[4]

---

[1] R. A. Caminos, *Buhen*, i, p. 59, qui ajoute que le graffite 'was written when the block has been dislodged from its place in the door-jamb'.

[2] Caminos, loc. cit.; illustration pl. 70, 1 (dessin); pl. 69, 1 (vue générale).

[3] Un problème subsiste pourtant pour la dernière lettre. Sayce y voyait le signe qu'il transcrivait *vu* (d'où *vu* chez

Bork-Friedrich). Ševoroškin, *Issledovanija*, p. 311, 83–84 Š, etc., a transcrit par *b* (différent de B, pour lui *b₁*). Je suppose aujourd'hui qu'il s'agit de N d'orientation sinistroverse, employés à côté de N qui sont dextroverses, contrairement au sens des deux graffites; voir § 8, sous *11*.

[4] R. A. Caminos, *Buhen*, i, p. 71 (mention du graffite, sans reproduction).

Ce graffite, copié par Sayce en 1893–1894, a été retrouvé à Khartoum en 1962 par R. A. Caminos; le tambour de colonne avait été déposé en 1910 et envoyé dans le musée, où il se trouve toujours.[1] Le graffite carien est assez légèrement incisé sur les cinq pans du tambour; plusieurs signes sont de lecture difficile.

△ A M ⋀ ⌇ Ⅎ ⊐

Φ Ⅎ ⊖ A ⏘ ⊖ ⊓ O V ⋀

Đ X ⏀ X A ⊐ ⋀ Ⅎ V

(1) *27-é-ṃ-s-a-d*   (2) *m-ụ-o-27-25 | a-25-v-25*   (3) *u-v-ṣ-27̣-a-ḥ-29-h-ẹ*

L. 1. D'abord un rectangle, probablement *27*; ensuite *é* certain, avec quatre branches vers la gauche; puis deux signes de structure M, une séquence *ṃ-s* semblant la plus probable. Peut-être un mot en *s-a-d*, comme en **50** et **51**?

L. 2. La copie de Sayce est à peu près confirmée, sauf pour le s. 2 qui est plutôt un *u*. On a probablement deux mots.

L. 3. Apparemment un seul mot de neuf signes, commençant par *u-v-s* (voir un mot à début comparable dans **7**) et se terminant par *h-e*.

Il est dommage que cette inscription assez longue ne soit pas mieux conservée.

[1] Je remercie M. Caminos, qui m'a signalé la présence de la pierre et m'a fourni tous les renseignements désirables, ainsi que les autorités du Musée de Khartoum et M. André Vila, grâce à qui j'ai pu obtenir les excellentes photographies reproduites ici.

PART II

HIEROGLYPHIC STELAE WITH CARIAN TEXTS AND CARIAN STELAE WITH EGYPTIANIZING OR HELLENIZING MOTIFS

BY

GEOFFREY THORNDIKE MARTIN

Lecturer in Egyptology
University College London

AND

RICHARD VAUGHAN NICHOLLS

Senior Keeper, Department of Antiquities
Fitzwilliam Museum, Cambridge

INTRODUCTION

THE stelae dealt with in the following commentary[1] fall into three groups:

(a) No. **2**. A stela made by an Egyptian or foreign craftsman, bearing hieroglyphic inscriptions with Carian text added later. The upper part of the stela is missing, and would probably have been decorated with reliefs. Commentary by G. T. Martin.

(b) Nos. **1, 7**. Stelae with contemporary Egyptian and Carian texts. Commentary by G. T. Martin.

(c) Nos. **3, 4, 5, 5a, 6**. Stelae made by foreign (probably Carian) craftsmen, bearing reliefs that are either Egyptianizing or in a provincial East Greek style and, with one exception, Carian inscriptions. Commentaries by G. T. Martin and R. V. Nicholls.

In the discussion certain common iconographic and other details are dealt with at somewhat greater length than is usually necessary in an Egyptological publication. This is because it is recognized that the present volume will be consulted by scholars whose interests are not primarily Egyptological.[2]

The account of the non-Egyptian scenes on nos. **3, 4, 5** and **5a** by R. V. Nicholls offers an exciting glimpse of the art, dress, and beliefs of the Carian community at Memphis in the second half of the sixth century B.C. The stylistic antecedents of the provincial art so revealed are patently East Greek, although the craftsmen involved were also artistically bilingual, and adopted Egyptian conventions when showing Egyptian religious scenes. The development of Caromemphite, Hellenomemphite, and early Persomemphite stelae is discussed, as well as the significance of the Memphite *prothesis* scenes and the work of the 'Saqqâra Master'. The republication of the closely related stela from Abûsîr (Berlin, Aegyptisches Museum 19553), which has now also been re-identified as Caromemphite, has been arranged by the kindness of Dr. Steffen Wenig and of the Staatliche Museen in Berlin.[3]

---

[1] G. T. Martin wishes to thank Professor H. S. Smith, who showed him his unpublished preliminary report which dealt with all but one of the documents (No. 2), and Dr. R. D. Barnett, Mr. Brian Cook, and Professor H. De Meulenaere, who responded generously in the search for non-Egyptian parallels to the prothesis scenes in Nos. **4, 5**, and **5a**. Some of the bibliographical references are utilized by R. V. Nicholls in his account of these scenes.

[2] In general, no provenances or measurements are given, since these are mentioned by O. Masson in Part I of this volume.

[3] Here, pl. xxx (photograph courtesy of the Staatliche Museen, Berlin). See the commentary by R. V. Nicholls in the section concerning **3**, and for the inscription, Appendice I by O. Masson.

THE STELAE

1. H5-1349 Plates I, 1; II, 1; XXXI, 1

This monument consists of the upper part of a round-topped limestone stela, of which an upper register, one line of incised hieroglyphic inscription, and two lines of Carian text (both texts between borders) survive, together with the remains of a second register (see p. 20 above).

Much of the surface of the top portion of the fragment is damaged. Originally, the lunette contained a sun-disk (now missing) with pendent wings, the latter undecorated. Above and following the line of the wings are traces which doubtless represent the remains of the greatly elongated sign for 'heaven' (☰), present, for example, on many of the votive stelae from the Serapeum.[1]

The scene in the first register shows the owner of the stela advancing from the right, with both hands raised in the traditional gesture of adoration, the recipient of which is a seated figure of the god Osiris. The deceased is wearing a bag-wig, bead-collar, and full kilt fastened at the waist by a band. He wears a transverse linen band over his right shoulder in the manner of Egyptian lector-priests.[2] The eye and ear only are shown in outline, and no attempt is made to render the details of the lips and nose, the figures of the deities on the same stela being accorded similar treatment.

The seated mummiform figure of Osiris is shown wearing the White Crown of Upper Egypt with double plumes, with a uraeus at the brow. The thin ceremonial beard at the chin is very summarily rendered, and the curled tip is not shown. Around his neck is a bead collar. He holds the ḥeḳa(t)-sceptre in his left hand, and grasps the *nekhakha*-flail in his right. The handles, which are usually shown passing in front of the torso, are not depicted. The side of the throne of Osiris, which is mounted on a pedestal in the form of the hieroglyphic sign *maʿat*, 'Truth', is decorated with a design of diminishing rectangles, and over the low back is a cushion or cloth.

Between Osiris and the deceased is a tall stand with a triangular opening in the base, supporting a tray bearing a duck and three loaves. The bottom of the offering-table stands free of the base-line, probably for reasons of space. Behind Osiris is a standing figure of the goddess Isis, feet slightly apart, her left arm raised in a ritual gesture of protection, her right hand held at her side and grasping the sign of 'Life' (*ʿankh*). Isis wears a tripartite wig, one lappet of which falls over her right shoulder, surmounted by a diadem on which is mounted a solar disk flanked by cows' horns. Her close-fitting dress is tied at the waist, and is supported by a strap passing over the left shoulder. A collar of beads can be seen at her neck.

An incised legend enclosed within a rectangular frame is shown in front of the two deities. Before Osiris we read: *Words spoken by Osiris*, and before Isis: *Words spoken by Isis*.

These abbreviated formulae stand in lieu of a full recitation or utterance on the part of the deities, and neither exhibits any orthographic or other peculiarity.

Before the face of the stela-owner is a rectangle containing an inscription which, in view of its

---

[1] Cf. for instance, J. Vercoutter, *Textes biographiques du Sérapéum de Memphis* (Paris, 1962), pls. III, IV, VI–IX, XIII, XIX; M. Malinine, G. Posener, J. Vercoutter, *Catalogue des stèles du Sérapéum de Memphis*, i, Plate vol. (Paris, 1968), nos. 22, 23, 25, 32, 35, 36, 53, 76, 89, 90, 129, 148, 149, 152, 155, 192, 194, 213; G. Posener, *La Première domination perse en Égypte* (Cairo, 1936), pl. III. The representation of the firmament occurs alone or in conjunction with the winged disk.

[2] Cf. E. Staehelin, *Untersuchungen zur ägyptischen Tracht im Alten Reich* (Berlin, 1966), 80–4.

position and determinative, can only be the owner's name, reading from right to left, *Mrš(ꜣ)*.[1] This name, which is not cited in Ranke, *Personennamen*, is probably foreign.

The vertical incised legend over the offering-table presents a problem. The beginning is lost, apart from a minute trace, and part of the penultimate sign is destroyed. The enclosing border has no base-line. The inscription appears to read:

$$\text{𝖄𝕯𝖄 . . . } mrymꜣ(?)$$

This may refer to the offerings, or it may be a personal name. The traces of the penultimate sign could also be ⸗ or even ⸗. The last sign is almost certainly an *aleph* rather than a *sꜣ*-sign (𓅬). The latter would have suggested a filiation sign, the text then reading: . . . *mrymꜣ* (?)[2] son of *Mrš(ꜣ)*.

There is no 'seated-man' determinative at the end of the first 'name', as one would expect on the analogy of the second, but there are many precedents for such an omission, which could be due to lack of space. I have little confidence in the reading of the first 'name' as it stands.

The line of hieroglyphs beneath the upper register call for little comment. The text reads, from right to left, referring to the scene above: *Words spoken by Osiris, foremost of the Westerners: he grants a goodly burial in the necropolis.*

Certain palaeographic and other peculiarities may be noted:

1. The *n* of the invocation *ḏd mdw in* is omitted.
2. The summary form of *ḫntt* (𓊈). The position of the second ⸗ of *ḫntt* is only very faintly marked.
3. The omission of the base of the sarcophagus-sign in *ḳrs(t)*, and the writing of ⸗ (presumably) beneath it.

Very little survives of the scene in the second register. It is clear that the traces represent the upheld wing and arm of the goddess Isis, protecting an image of the Apis Bull,[3] whose name, *Ḥp* is written in hieroglyphs above. The feather of *maꜥat*, 'Truth', is held aloft in the goddess's hand.[4] Presumably, the lost part of this scene showed either the ibis-headed Thoth,[5] or the stela-owner[6] worshipping the Apis, and on the analogy of related stelae it seems probable that there was yet another register below, depicting the deceased or a relative on a funerary bier surrounded by mourners. This means that approximately only half the original stela survives. It seems more doubtful whether, on the analogy of other stelae in the series, another inscription in Carian was inscribed between registers 2 and 3, in view of the fact that boldly incised texts in both hieroglyphic and Carian are present between registers 1 and 2, but the possibility cannot be ruled out.

Since the stela displays orthodox iconography, palaeography, and orthography from the Egyptian point of view, it seems virtually certain that it was executed by a native Egyptian craftsman. The Carian text is exactly contemporary, indicated by the fact that both inscriptions are an integral part of the superimposed registers, with Egyptian again occurring in the second register, below. The Carian, which is well cut, could have been the work of a separate craftsman, or of a skilled

---

[1] J. R. Baines suggested to H. S. Smith that ⸗ might perhaps be written for ⸗ *i(w)*, as sometimes in Ptolemaic hieroglyphs. The name might then read: *Irš* (or *Iršꜣ*), for which cf. 7, below. H. De Meulenaere refers me to the name Τμαρσις, which corresponds to *Tꜣ-mrš* in demotic, cf. Möller, *Mumienschilder*, 13. [2] Or . . . *mry-tꜣwy* (?). [3] Cf. 4, 5, 5a, 6. [4] Cf. 4, 5. [5] Cf. 4, 5, 5a. [6] Cf. 6 = H5-1222.

native Egyptian sculptor. In view of its position one would expect the Carian to be a translation of, or at least to convey the meaning of, the Egyptian text.

Stylistically, the stela dates to the Twenty-sixth or Twenty-seventh dynasties.

2. H5-1703 + H5-1006   Plates I, 2; XXXI, 2

These two limestone fragments were found in different seasons, and were catalogued and numbered separately. The fragment H5-1703 was excavated in the 1969–70 season, in débris on the east side of the 'South Screen Wall'[1] of the main Temple complex, which adjoins the sacred animal catacombs, and was copied by J. R. Baines. An additional facsimile was made by the present writer in February 1973. The fragment consists of the lower part of a stela, of which the left side and part of the base have original surfaces. The upper portion and right half are lacking.

The text consists of the ends of two horizontal registers of incised hieroglyphs between borders, reading from right to left, with the remains of two[2] lines of incised Carian inscription underneath (see p. 21 above), and a roughly scratched line below. An additional feature, placed below the Carian text and towards the centre of the fragment, is a simple design consisting of a horizontal line with three uprights, resembling the hieroglyphic sign or determinative for 'hill-country' or 'foreign land' (ᴗᴗ). Further to the right and adjoining the edge of the fragment, is part of another sign, similar to the hieroglyphic letter *f* (ᕙ). A line of red pigment can be discerned above the last sign (ᗕ) in the first row of hieroglyphs. The hieroglyphic text is discussed below. The Carian inscription is more lightly incised, and an attempt has been made in antiquity to obliterate it. The signs are outlined in black.

Fragment H5-1006 was found in the 1968–9 season, in débris which had accumulated in front of the entrance to the Baboon Galleries. Presumably, it (and H5-1703) had been used for the blocking of the niches of baboon interments, like most of the Carian stelae found reused in the Sacred Animal Necropolis, and had been thrown out in the course of plundering. The fragment consists of the lower part of a stela, of which the upper and left-hand parts are missing. The surface is very badly worn and scratched, and no trace remains of any scene above. The inscriptions consist of the beginning of two horizontal registers of incised hieroglyphs between borders, reading from right to left. Below are the remains of a lightly incised Carian text. The Carian inscription has been partly obliterated, and the beginning of both lines is lost. The remaining characters are outlined in black.

Several indications suggest to the present writer that both fragments are part of the same stela.

1. Each fragment is about half the width of an average stela.
2. The borders separating the registers, including the line under the Carian text, coincide exactly.
3. The hieroglyphic and Carian texts in both fragments consist of two lines only in each case.
4. The joined hieroglyphic texts make good sense.
5. The treatment of the Carian inscription is the same in both cases.
6. The thickness of both fragments is the same (5·0 cms).

It should be noted that the border faintly marked in red pigment above the upper register in H5-1703 is not now present in H5-1006, and has doubtless weathered away. The surface condition

[1] Now called the 'East enclosure wall'.
[2] A note on the field catalogue card of H5-1703 suggests that the remains of three lines of hieroglyphic inscription were present, but re-examination has shown that the 'sign' above ᗕ, present in the original facsimile copy, is illusory.

of the latter has been remarked upon above. In H5–1006 an incised border at a higher level can be discerned.

Most of the Egyptian text is unremarkable, the joined fragments consisting of part of a standard funerary invocation: *A boon which the king gives (to) Ptah–Sokar . . . [lord of?] heaven, king of the gods, ruler of Eternity, that he may give a [goodly] burial . . .*[1]

The ends of both lines of text are blundered. The end of the first is probably to be interpreted as [*nb*] *pt*, 'lord of heaven', the *pt*-sign being clear, the 'signs' before and below being meaningless. The signs at the end of the second line are clearly an attempt to render the words *ḳrs(t) nfr(t)* 'goodly burial'.

The Egyptian inscription was never finished, the text apparently not being carried over into a third line. The work may be that of an illiterate scribe imperfectly copying an existing inscription, or it may be the product of a foreign craftsman not wholly familiar with Egyptian hieroglyphs. The maladroit writing of the ends of the text could have been the reason why the stela was abandoned and not used for its original purpose. Equally, it may have been an example of a mass-produced inscription from a funerary workshop, awaiting the title and name of a customer.

The Carian text was evidently added later, and subsequently an attempt was made to erase it. The hieroglyphic text is probably of the Twenty-sixth–Twenty-seventh dynasties.

Other orthographic and epigraphic peculiarities which call for comment are:

1. In the writing of the *ḥtp di nsw* formula, the △ and ⌒ are transposed.
2. The cutting of the ⌐ sign, with the hook at the top separate from the handle, is unusual. The trace of the determinative under *ḍ* has a flat base, and is presumably for ⌒, cf. *Wb*, iii, 170.
3. The remains of the word *ḏt* can be discerned on H5–1703, the full writing being ⌐, cf. *Wb*, iii, 172, 19.
4. The pronoun *f* in *di·f* is clumsily written.

3. H5–1229   Plates II, 2; III; XXXII

The limestone of this stela is characterized by fossil inclusions, and the resultant pittings were apparently originally plugged with plaster. Parts of the face of the stela have flaked away, and there are also remains of mortar from its subsequent reuse adhering to parts of its face and edges.

The technique of decoration approximates more to Greek incised drawing than to relief, but there is, in fact, also very shallow modelling over the main surfaces, after the fashion of Egyptian recessed relief. All colour has vanished. The rounded top of the stela is occupied by a winged sun-disk with uraei, rendered after the Egyptian fashion. The heads of the cobras hang poised to either side of the disk and their tails trail along the leading edge of the wings. The wings curve downwards, following the shape of the top of the stela. The feathers are incised, the primaries having angled tips, but the secondaries and longer coverts being rendered as simple incised stripes. A scale pattern is used to indicate the shorter coverts at the front of the wings.

The rest of the decoration of the stela is wholly un-Egyptian. Beneath the winged sun-disk two figures stand facing each other, both some 51 cm. high and both rendered in a sort of provincial East Greek style, with vertical Carian inscriptions behind their backs (see p. 22 above). Because the surface preservation makes it difficult to follow their rendering at some points, let alone interpret

---

[1] Cf. **1**.

the artistic conventions involved, these figures will be described in some detail in the account that follows. The base line on which they stand is not single, but fourfold. Four parallel incised horizontal lines seem originally to have run right across the stela. These lines are rather too close together to represent any form of architectural stepping and may be little more than the incised frame for a broad band of colour or colours. Beneath, the face of the stela seems to have been completely plain.

The figure to the left is that of a woman with her left hand outstretched to her companion's chin, and her right hand clasped by him at the wrist. She is dressed in a long, crinkly, pleated linen *chiton* and a woollen cloak, worn as a veil over the back of her head. The *chiton* trails on the ground behind in a conventionalized flaring curve. It also has a large fold, or *kolpos*, hanging down in front, where the surplus material has been tucked up over the girdle. Other stelae published below, showing the women in a similar *chiton* but without a cloak, indicate that the *kolpos* was worn only in front and that it was probably a device for hoisting the hem of the trailing garment clear of the feet.[1] The pleating of the linen is indicated by parallel incised wavy lines. These are absent over the breast, but this need not indicate so much a change in the material as that it is here much more amply filled! The outer edges of the sleeves of the *chiton* are shown just below the edge of the cloak, above the elbows. The lady's cloak is a woollen *himation* worn over her back, with its middle part brought up over the back of her head as a veil. Its two top corners hang down over her shoulders inside her upper arms. Where these corners hang down in front, incised lines show that two broad stripes ran along the top edge of the cloak.[2] These are probably to be understood as tucked under where the cloak forms the veil over the lady's head. The incised band framing her face is much narrower and is rather to be interpreted as the edge of the kind of under-veil often appearing in East Greek art in this period. This conceals her hair and ears apart from a few strands of hair which escape just below ear level. Her feet are poorly preserved. Most probably they were together and the faint trace of a sole-line suggests that they were shod.

Despite faintly androgynous touches in the soft modelling of his body, her companion is definitely a man. He is shown standing, with his right leg advanced and with his left hand gripping the lady's right wrist and his right hand outstretched to her chin. His feet also are ill preserved. They seem to have been large and rather wedge-shaped and part of his advanced right foot was apparently hidden behind the feet of the woman. He wears a thin linen *chiton* reaching down to his lower calves, but leaving his ankles bare, and with sleeves extending almost to his elbows. It seems nearly transparent—at least his legs and left arm are rendered as showing clearly through it, although it is significant that there seems to have been no attempt to indicate the genitals. The bottom edge of the *chiton* is marked by a broad, opaque hem or stripe. The right sleeve is also, doubtless accidentally, rendered as opaque. It also carries incised lines indicating the folds radiating from a button or pin fastening it a little below the shoulder. Over his *chiton* the man wears a short woollen cloak, or *chlamys*, with double stripes down its side edge and triple stripes along its top. This seems to be worn with its top third folded back double and with this folded edge drawn about the man's shoulders. Its left corner is draped over his left upper arm and hangs well down on the inside of the arm. Its right corner has been brought up over between his neck and right shoulder, leaving his right arm free. This corner hangs much higher and juts forward awkwardly from his chest, curiously echoing the lady's voluminous breast. At this point the edges of the two thicknesses of material

---

[1] See below, pp. 71 f, 81 f, 84 f.

[2] Subsequent damage, in the form of surface scratches, gives the false appearance of a greater number of stripes below the right elbow.

folded together are shown as separating over the shoulder—at least this seems the most logical interpretation for the lines as incised, since to regard them as part of a zigzag fold would be quite out of keeping with the conservative drawing. The wool of the *chlamys* seems also to have been intended as very thin and light. For, although the stripes at the edges are rendered as opaque, the left arm, leg, and buttock are indicated as showing through the cloak.

The man's hair is worn full, but leaves the ear exposed and is trimmed off abruptly at the nape of the neck. Indeed, it is a hair-style that it is very hard to match in Greek art of the period to which the drawing would seem to belong.[1] But, on the other hand, it corresponds quite closely with the form of contemporary Egyptian wigs. The oblique cross-hatching with which the hair is rendered may strengthen the view that a wig is intended, since the natural stranding of live hair would hang very differently. And, if this is the case, it is the one significant concession that these figures make to Egyptian fashion. As compared with the delicate rendering of the woman's face, the man's head seems, at first sight, awkward and ugly. This is largely due to surface damage, which has obliterated the lower lip, and a resultant optical effect which, in many lights, makes it seem as if the mouth was set higher than is actually the case. There is another curious feature to be recorded in connection with the treatment of the man's face, but in this case it is no longer completely clear how far this is part of the original decoration and how far it is the product of subsequent damage. The lower part of the man's face is covered with a pitting or stippling, and this would seem to stop on a line that curves round from just under the nose up to the 'sideboard' of the wig. In other words, he may have been wearing a short beard and moustache. This would accord well enough with East Greek practice, but strikes a slightly incongruous note combined, as here, with what seems to be an Egyptian wig—unless, of course, he is simply wearing the stubble allowed to accumulate while in mourning, and thus being identified as the bereaved.

Some guidance as to date is provided by comparing the figures with East Greek art. Especially striking are the resemblances existing between the delicately rendered head of the lady and south Ionian marble sculptures of the middle and third quarter of the sixth century B.C.[2] The flat treatment of the drapery on both figures and the absence of any naturalistic rendering of the folds would also normally tend to confirm a date no later than this. Indeed, at first sight, the formal pleating of the woman's *chiton* and its trumpet-like flare at the bottom might seem to command comparison with works of the second quarter of the century.[3] That the stela is later, however, than these seems to be indicated by the clear separate articulation of the garments and there are also significant differences in the actual garments themselves. Thus the lady's deep *kolpos* in front is quite different in function not only from both the short *himation* and the *apoptygma*, or overfold, of the earlier statues, but also from the shallow *kolpos* at each side, hanging down when the arms are lowered, as on Geneleos' statues and related works. There are also other features that seem rather old-fashioned or, more probably, deliberately mannered in a time-range extending from the mid sixth century B.C. These include the curiously elongated proportions of the figures and the extremely formal character of the gestures of endearment. These last have more the flavour of the seventh century B.C.[4] and seem here a definitely mannerist feature.

[1] The author has also referred (*Arch. Reports*, 1970–1, 76) to a conservative hairstyle of similar length that seems to persist into the sixth century B.C. on the Carian terracottas from Alazeytin; but the present hair treatment seems much closer to Egyptian wigs.

[2] Cf. G. M. A. Richter, *Korai, Archaic Greek Maidens* (London, 1968), 59–60 nos. 94–8, figs. 291–300, 304–5.

[3] Ibid. 44–54, 'Cheramyes-Geneleos Group', especially nos. 55–62, figs. 183–206.

[4] Cf. scene on Cretan vase from Afrati: *Ann. Sc. It. Atene* 10–12 (1927–9), 339–41, figs. 443 *a–d*, pl. 23; *Hesperia* 14 (1945), 24, pl. 16.

But the closest parallels for this work are to be found in certain other limestone stelae also from Egypt showing, to varying degrees, a similar provincial Greek style and mostly executed in a similar technique, somewhere between Egyptian shallow recessed relief and Greek incised drawing. These are almost all from the vicinity of Memphis and, indeed, the biggest discovery of these consists of the examples found together with the present stela and published in this volume. They are quite different in character from the few local Greek reliefs from the Greek trading settlement at Naucratis in the Delta and they were probably all executed at Memphis itself by resident alien craftsmen. Their foreign inscriptions are in Carian or, later, in the Persian Period, Aramaic. The Carian examples preponderate, but one hesitates to describe the art of these stelae as specifically Carian, since it is by no means clear whether, in the second half of the sixth century B.C., one can speak of a distinctively Carian style, as against that of southern East Greece, and after centuries of East Greek cultural influence in Caria.[1] The stelae do, however, show certain fairly consistent peculiarities of dress and, in the case of the *prothesis* scenes, of ritual. The dress of the figures is basically Greek; its distinctive features are the long trailing *chiton* of the women with its deep *kolpos* in front and the thin, nearly transparent, sleeved *chiton* of the men reaching to mid calf. But these seem more likely to be local Memphite variations due to the Egyptian climate, the ready availability of fine linen and, possibly, the special status of the local foreign community. The ritual peculiarity consists in the combination of elements from the funerary banquet with the laying out of the dead. But here both of the features combined are wholly Greek in both conception and iconography.

The stelae themselves fall into three different groups. To Group A belong:

A1. The present stela, now Cambridge inv. no. E.1.1971. Carian inscriptions.

A2. East Berlin inv. no. 19553 (also numbered 24139),[2] *prothesis* stela from Abûsîr (pl. XXX). R. Zahn in L. Borchardt, *Das Grabdenkmal des Königs Saᵌḥureᶜ*, i (Leipzig, 1910), 135–7, fig. 187; W. Zschietzschmann in *Ath. Mitt.* 53 (1928), 32, 44, no. 94, Beil. 16; Fr. W. von Bissing, 'Totenstele eines persischen Großen aus Memphis', *ZDMG* 84 (NF 9, 1930), 226–38, especially 237, pl. 7; B. Porter and R. L. B. Moss, *Topographical Bibliography*, iii (Oxford, 1931), 83; J. Boardman, *The Greeks Overseas* (Harmondsworth, 1964), 152–3, pl. 9a; M. M. Austin, *Greece and Egypt in the Archaic Age* (Cambridge, 1970), 57; K. Parlasca in *Staatl. Mus. zu Berlin, Forschungen und Berichte* 14 (1972), 76 (where further bibliography), pl. 5, 2. Ill-preserved inscription, probably Carian, but hitherto misread as Greek; see Appendice I (O. Masson).

The figures on both these stelae show similar elongated and rather mannered proportions. Such proportions are otherwise not entirely unknown in Greek work in Egypt, being occasionally met with rather earlier at Naucratis in some of the statuettes carved locally in Egyptian limestone and alabaster.[3] The woman at the head of the bier on the Berlin stela and the lady on that in Cambridge both seem to wear similar veils with similar escaping shoulder-locks. And many other resemblances in body modelling suggest themselves between the man on the Cambridge stela and the man at the foot of the couch on that in Berlin. The heads of the figures on the Berlin stela are proportionately

[1] e.g. already in Protogeometric and Geometric times: V. R. d'A. Desborough, *Protogeometric Pottery* (Oxford, 1952), 218–21; idem, *The Greek Dark Ages* (London, 1972), 179–83; J. N. Coldstream, *Greek Geometric Pottery* (London, 1968), 263, 268, 296–7, 339, 377.

[2] Republished here by permission of the Staatliche Museen and through the good offices of Dr. S. Wenig, who has also helped by providing photographs and rubbings of the inscription. Dr. L. H. Jeffery was the first to suggest, in correspondence, that the inscription had previously been read upside down and was probably Carian, as Dr Martin suspected. Preserved finished edges at right and bottom; broken surface at top and along most of left edge; it is thus not entirely to be excluded that this stela may once have had upper registers like those of Group B below. See p. 91.

[3] e.g. F. N. Pryce, *BMC Greek and Roman Sculpture*, i, Part 1 (London, 1928), 183–4 no. B 438, pl. 39; G. M. A. Richter, *Kouroi, Archaic Greek Youths* (3rd ed., London and New York, 1970), 57–8, no. 28, figs. 129–30.

larger and more angular. In this they offer some limited points of resemblance with the only significant known East Greek grave relief near the ostensible time-range of these stelae, the relief from Chalcedon in Istanbul, which is probably to be dated towards the middle of the sixth century B.C.[1] It is of interest to note in passing how the extremely shallow cutting of the Istanbul relief also produces an emphasis on line and a kind of flat modelling that must likewise originally have depended heavily on painting for its finished effect. Among Greek work from Egypt, a somewhat analogous kind of carving seems attested on Greek reliefs from Naucratis.[2]

The two stelae of Group A show no Egyptian features in their broad design apart from the winged sun-disk, and are otherwise in a curious local provincial East Greek style. They show marked differences in style and proportions from those of Group B which, as will be seen below, seem broadly datable to about the last quarter of the sixth century B.C. They show many features that seem earlier than the Group B stelae but, on internal evidence, seem unlikely to be much earlier than the mid-sixth century B.C. So they are here assigned provisionally to about the third quarter of the sixth century B.C. Within this time-range the old-fashioned Cambridge stela may be earlier than that in Berlin, which already also looks forward to the later British Museum stela, B1 below.

The Group B stelae are all from the recent excavations at Saqqâra and are all published here:

B1. Saqqâra, now British Museum 67235; below, no. **4**, pl. IV, 1. Carian inscription, probably added after carving complete.

B2. Saqqâra; below, no. **5a**, pl. V, 2. Uninscribed.

B3. Saqqâra; below, no. **5**, pl. V, 1. Carian inscription, probably added after carving complete.

These three stelae are remarkably consistent in both style and type. All have winged sun-disks above and three registers of decoration below, the two uppermost with the same Egyptian religious scenes rendered more or less according to Egyptian conventions yet unmistakably by craftsmen whose normal idiom was provincial Greek. On all three stelae the bottom register is occupied by a scene wholly in a provincial East Greek style showing the *prothesis*, or laying out, of a corpse.

It is argued below that the form of the couch on the British Museum stela, B1, indicates a date hardly much earlier than the last quarter of the sixth century B.C., and other indications on the other two stelae tend to confirm this.[3] On the other hand, the conservative treatment of the drapery in all three *prothesis* scenes still echoes the conventions of the third quarter of the century and would seem, despite the provinciality of the style, to discount a date any later than the last quarter of the century. Such conclusions are confirmed by the dating of the stelae of the succeeding phase, Group C, discussed below, and by the known existence at Memphis of a much more advanced local archaic Greek style, ostensibly of around 500 B.C. This is best attested in a large limestone statuette of a goddess from Memphis, again a local work in a provincial East Greek style.[4] Whether the earlier-looking of the two painted wooden panels from Saqqâra showing Greek influence is to be included under this head seems much more doubtful.[5] This shows a procession with a cow and a bull; although its style reveals vestigial late archaic traits, e.g. in the rendering of the hands, its execution should be no earlier than the mid fifth century B.C., to judge from the Greek dress of the woman awaiting the oncoming procession.

[1] G. Mendel, *Cat. des Sculptures, Mus. Roy. Ott.* ii (Istanbul, 1914), 227–8 no. 524 (where earlier bibliography); L. H. Jeffery in *BSA* 50 (1955), 81–3, pl. 10*a*; B. Schmaltz in *Ist. Mitt.* 19–20 (1969–70), 177–85, pl. 33 (where further bibliography).

[2] C. C. Edgar in *BSA* 5 (1898–9), 65–7, pl. 9 (cf. ibid. 33); id. in *JHS* 25 (1905), 126–7, fig. 8; Pryce, op. cit. 180–1, no.

B 437, fig. 220.

[3] p. 75; cf. also pp. 82, 84 f.

[4] C. C. Edgar, *Cat. Cairo, Greek Sculpture* (Cairo, 1903), 3–4, no. 27431, pl. 1.

[5] *JEA* 57 (1971), 10–11, fig. 3; a better idea of the painting can be formed from the colour reproduction used as frontispiece to G. T. Martin, *Tomb of Ḥetepka* (London, 1978).

The British Museum example, B1, is manifestly the finest of the three stelae of Group B. The other two, B2 and B3, seem very closely related to each other and are, in fact, assigned in their detailed discussion to the same artist, there named the Saqqâra Master. Although their iconography is clearly linked with that of the British Museum stela, they seem, when set against it, to be much humbler derivative versions of the same theme. The final degradation of the type may possibly be represented by a fourth Saqqâra stela with a Carian inscription published in this volume.[1] This omits the *prothesis* scene altogether and substitutes the person commemorated for Thoth in the second register, but it seems nevertheless still to show stylistic connections with the stelae of Group B and with the work of the Saqqâra Master himself. The resemblances between all these stelae are strong enough to suggest that the whole development may have covered a relatively short period of time and thus may have fallen entirely in the last quarter of the sixth century B.C.

Unlike the foregoing, Group C is not a homogeneous unit and simply serves to bring together some of the other alien, but non-Carian, Memphite stelae of late archaic Greek date that show possible links with the Carian examples of Groups A and B above—a Graeco-Persian relief and two examples from the larger class of local Egypto-Phoenician stelae,[2] the one because it also shows elements of Graeco-Persian style and the other because it provides a precise date for a somewhat similar type of representation. As will be seen below, other local Egypto-Phoenician stelae group themselves around these last two examples. The three stelae that thus seem most relevant for consideration here are the following:

C1. East Berlin inv. no. 23721, stela showing the *prothesis* of a Persian dignitary in 'Median' dress, from Memphis. Von Bissing, op. cit. 226–38, pl. 1; Parlasca, op. cit. 76 n. 22 (where full bibliography), pl. 3, 1. Uninscribed.

C2. Vatican inv. no. 287, stela of ʿAnkh-ḥap, of unrecorded provenance. G. Botti and P. Romanelli, *Le sculture del Museo Gregoriano Egizio* (Vatican, 1951), 90–1, no. 135, pl. 62; von Bissing, op. cit. 230–1, pl. 3. Aramaic inscription: *CIS* 2, no. 142, pl. 14.

C3. East Berlin inv. no. 7707, stela of Abah and Akhatbu, from Saqqâra. K. R. Lepsius in *ZÄS* 15 (1877), 127–32, pl. 1; *ZÄS* 49 (1911), 73–4, pl. 8; von Bissing, op. cit. 230, pl. 2. Aramaic and hieroglyphic inscriptions: *CIS* 2, no. 122, pl. 11; P. Grelot, *Documents araméens d'Égypte* (1972), 341–2, no. 85. Dated 482 B.C.

These stelae present a curious and varying blend of Achaemenid, Phoenician, Greek, and Egyptian elements and command attention here because of the iconographic links between the first of them and the Carian *prothesis* stelae of Groups A and B above. The style of the first two claims comparison not only with the Persepolis reliefs but also with the early Graeco-Persian grave reliefs from Daskylion and elsewhere in Asia Minor,[3] and, like them, these two are carved in raised relief, while the third, C3, is in Egyptian sunk relief.

The *prothesis* stela, C1, shows an essentially Greek concept rendered in a Graeco-Persian style. The inclusion of a table beside the bier is a particularly significant feature, otherwise only known from Memphis and then only on the stelae, A2 and B1 above. It is thus tempting to postulate some small overlap in date between this stela and those of Group B with *prothesis* scenes and so assign it

---

[1] Below, no. 6, pl. IV, 2, also with a Carian inscription; on p. 82 f. treated as 'near the Saqqâra Master'.

[2] Doubtless, the monuments of the Memphite Phoenicians of Herodotus II, 112. A Phoenician stela from Saqqâra apparently even earlier than those considered here and assigned to the sixth century B.C. on epigraphical grounds seems to show a corpse laid out on a couch, possibly under the inspiration of the Carian *prothesis* stelae, although there are no traces of Greek style: E. Lipiński, 'La stèle égypto-

araméenne de Tumma', in *Chron. d'Ég.* 50 (1975), 93–104, fig. 1. For fuller bibliography on the Memphite Egypto-Phoenician stelae, ibid. 93–4; the writer is indebted to Professor Masson and Dr. Martin, for bibliographical help.

[3] Most usefully assembled in J. Borchardt, 'Epichorische, gräkopersisch beeinflußte Reliefs in Kilikien', in *Ist. Mitt.* 18 (1968), 161–211, pls. 40–57. For heads of main mourners of C2, cf. Saqqâra *shabti*, K. Parlasca in *Wandlungen* (Waldsassen, 1975), 59, pl. 10 *b–c*.

still to the late sixth century B.C. It equally cannot be much earlier than this because the treatment of the beard and 'Median' dress of the dead dignitary and the curving profile of his horse's head already show the influence of the new conventions developed under Darius I from 518 B.C. on for the decoration of the royal buildings at Persepolis. Indeed, a date earlier than *c*. 510 B.C. is probably precluded for the Memphis stela. Equally, it may not be much later, to judge from the furniture shown. Both couch and table are of West Asiatic varieties, but they are both markedly different from the furniture appearing on the Persepolis reliefs and typologically earlier than this, still showing lingering resemblances to representations on Late Assyrian reliefs of the late eighth and seventh centuries B.C. and to the contemporary Assyrianizing art of Syria and the rest of the Levant.[1] Apart from the *prothesis*, other Greek features include the mourning sirens flanking the corpse.

The unprovenanced stela of ʿAnkh-ḥap, C2, has been plausibly assigned to Memphis on onomastic grounds. Its style and technique relate it to C1 and its iconography to C3. The *prothesis* has been replaced by a scene of Egyptian type, with the mummy on a lion-shaped embalming couch, analogous representations in raised relief recurring on the Carpentras and Salt stelae.[2] The mourners flanking the bier are shown in a Graeco-Persian style, the late archaic Greek character of their bearded heads suggesting a date in the early fifth century B.C.

On the stela of Abah and Akhatbu, C3, the lion-couch scenes have doubled and the style is more Egyptian in character. The fragmentary stela of Petisis from Saqqâra seems to have been rather similar and an uninscribed stela in Copenhagen in a partly un-Egyptian style repeats the scene with the mummy on a lion couch, but its ethnic associations are uncertain and its execution may have been much later, to judge from its possible 'neo-Memphite' echoes.[3]

The three stelae, C 1–3, would thus seem to have spanned the period, *c*. 510–482 B.C. and the whole development covered by Groups A, B, and C to have stretched between *c*. 550 B.C. (or a little later) and 482 B.C. It shows a conservative local East Greek style being used for Carian monuments and also adapting itself to Egyptian themes and conventions and eventually also influencing the art of other foreign communities at Memphis. All of these stelae were apparently produced at or near Memphis, the fossiliferous limestone characteristic of Groups A and B being possibly from Giza.[4]

To return now to the Cambridge stela, it has emerged from this discussion of the three groups that it is the earliest example of all, although it is unlikely to be earlier than the mid sixth century B.C. Still, if the Carian letter-forms can be any guide, a considerable gap in time may nevertheless separate it from the Group B stelae of the last quarter of the sixth century B.C., in which case a date early in the third quarter of the sixth century may not seem unreasonable. Other early mercenary dedications from Memphis seem to belong to much the same period.[5] Much interest attaches to the

[1] H. Kyrieleis, *Throne und Klinen* (*JDAI, Erg.* 25, 1969), 19, 148; cf. H. S. Baker, *Furniture in the Ancient World* (London, 1966), 183–203, 207–8, figs. 294–5, 303–6, 308, 332, 340.

[2] *CIS* 2, nos. 141, 143, pls. 13, 14; *PSBA* 26 (1904), 34–5, with pl.

[3] Petisis stela: *BIFAO* 38 (1939), 40–2 no. 14, pl. 3. Copenhagen stela: M. Mogensen, *La Glyptothèque Ny Carlsberg, la collection égyptienne* (Copenhagen, 1930), 105 no. A 758, pl. 113; O. Koefoed-Petersen, *Les stèles égyptiennes* (Copenhagen, 1948), 54–5, no. 71, pl. 71.

[4] Cf. A. Lucas, *Ancient Egyptian Materials and Industries*

(4th ed., revised by J. R. Harris, London, 1962), 53–4.

[5] e.g. Greek inscription from Memphis of third quarter of sixth century B.C. dedicating bronze to Theban Zeus (i.e. Amūn): *Cl. Rev.* 5 (1891), 77–8; L. H. Jeffery, *Local Scripts of Archaic Greece* (Oxford, 1961), 355, 358 no. 49, pl. 70; to be republished by O. Masson in *Revue d'Égyptologie*. Also, from recent excavations at North Saqqâra, head from a Naucratite alabaster *kouros* of *c*. 550–540 B.C., G 4–59 (5099), now Fitzwilliam Museum inv. no. GR.6.1975; close to Moscow *kouros* (Richter, *Kouroi*, 88 no. 82, figs. 264–6, where, however, dated too early, to judge from heads attached to Clazomenian vases).

closer determination of the date of the Cambridge stela because of the historical tradition that it was King Amasis (570–526 B.C.) who transferred the Ionian and Carian mercenaries to Memphis from Stratopeda.[1] It seems difficult not to associate the abrupt appearance at Memphis of the alien art of these stelae with this historical event. The surprising maturity shown by the Cambridge stela at the outset is more readily understandable if one may postulate an antecedent local East Greek and Carian tradition in the Delta—an assumption that also makes the many curiously old-fashioned features shown by the Cambridge stela more readily comprehensible. While it is impossible at this stage to say anything precise about this hypothetical antecedent local artistic tradition at Stratopeda, one may very reasonably expect it to be much older than that at Naucratis and, very probably, quite distinct from it. The art that developed from it after the transfer of the mercenaries to Memphis was presumably both Hellenomemphite and Caromemphite. The inscriptions on the stelae of Groups A and B discovered up to now are exclusively Carian, but it would seem premature to infer that they are distinctively Caromemphite, in view not only of their Greek style but also of the Greek practices and beliefs that they depict.

It does, however, seem likely that Ionian or Carian mercenaries may have been present in Memphis in smaller numbers for a considerable period before the transfer there of the main body of their compatriots.[2] A considerable amount of Greek pottery of the later seventh and sixth centuries B.C. has been found there, most of it having doubtless arrived via the new Greek trading station at Naucratis. But a few isolated Greek finds from Memphis and its vicinity seem to be earlier than the foundation of Naucratis. The most remarkable of these was discovered near the same temple in North Saqqâra as the present stela, and is likewise now in Cambridge. It is a Samian bronze griffon *protome* of *c.* 660 B.C., originally attached to a cauldron.[3] It would seem that an Ionian or Carian must have made the truly magnificent dedication of a Samian bronze griffon cauldron at the predecessor to this temple soon after the beginning of the reign of King Psammetichus I. But, at present, it seems that this earlier mercenary presence is attested only by imports and not by an indigenous Caromemphite or Hellenomemphite art of its own—an art which, as we have seen, may only have reached Memphis with the transfer of the main body of mercenaries there under Amasis.

It remains now to say something about the quite remarkable iconography of the Cambridge stela. It will not, of course, be possible to be dogmatic about the stela's function until its Carian inscriptions can be understood more completely. But, until then, it may most reasonably be presumed to have served to commemorate the dead, since this is unmistakably the role of the numerous Carian false-door stelae from Saqqâra and also, to judge from their *prothesis* scenes, of all the other stelae of Groups A and B discussed above. What is less clear is whether these stelae served as actual grave markers or were simply commemorative monuments set up, for example, at a sanctuary. No actual Carian cemetery has yet been discovered in the vicinity of the temple and galleries where they were found, and it also seems likely that the Egyptian scenes on the *prothesis* stelae may allude directly to the cults of the sacred area there. But, whether tombstones or commemorative votive

[1] Herodotus ii, 154; Diodorus i, 67. Cf. also O. Masson and J. Yoyotte, *Objets pharaoniques à inscription carienne* (Cairo, 1956), 2; Austin, *Greece and Egypt in Archaic Age*, 20–2, 56–8.

[2] For a summary of the pottery and other finds, see Austin, op. cit. 56–7; he relates this earlier presence of the mercenaries to the testimony of Polyaenus vii, 3.

[3] G 4–57 (5093), found in Cache 2, to the east of Mastaba 3518, with Egyptian bronzes of about the fourth and third centuries B.C., indicating the period by which the griffon cauldron had itself been destroyed; now Fitzwilliam Museum inv. no. GR.5.1975; it apparently falls towards the end of Jantzen's Group I of the cast *protomai*, for which see U. Jantzen, *Griechische Greifenkessel* (Berlin, 1955), 15–16, 54–6; contemporary with imported Egyptian bronzes in Samos (U. Jantzen, *Samos* viii (Bonn, 1972), 5–37, pls. 1–36).

monuments, these stelae seem to have been relegated to oblivion or menial reuse from the fourth century B.C. on, possibly, it has been suggested, because of some odium attaching to the Caromemphites, such as they might have incurred by supporting their Persian masters in the preceding struggles for Egyptian independence.[1]

Despite the extremely formal character of the gestures, the scene on the Cambridge stela achieves a kind of pathos. It would seem to show a tender farewell between a man and a woman, quite probably man and wife, and possibly both of them commemorated equally by the stela. If the function is funerary, then this is presumably the last farewell of all, the final parting between the living and the dead. Both figures are shown as alive and the separation is rendered as if one of the partners were simply leaving on a journey. In this, the Cambridge stela would seem to anticipate the conventions of the finest of Greek funerary art—that of Athens in the late fifth and fourth centuries B.C.— by over a century. Was this concept, of unique importance in the whole development of western art, then first evolved among the resident aliens of Memphis or, if it has local antecedents, in the mercenary camps of the Delta? No such problems, of course, arise with the *prothesis* scenes on the other stelae of Groups A and B, whose iconography, as will be seen below, finds ready antecedents in earlier existing Greek art, apart from certain interesting local details.[2]

It is, however, to be noted that the idea of the final farewell in its less literal and more poetic sense, as on the Cambridge stela, can be a verbal as well as a visual concept and there is thus no absolute need to postulate any direct *artistic* link between the present stela and the later grave reliefs of classical Athens. Also, although its iconography is a little confused and its execution, again, distinctly provincial, the stela from Chalcedon in Istanbul, cited earlier, shows a somewhat analogous scene, with the dead woman represented as alive, seated in a chair and surrounded by solicitous female relatives and servants. Again, the concept seems to anticipate Attic gravestones of the fourth century B.C. and, again, does such provincial work mark the first beginnings of these new ideas? As already remarked, the technique of the Istanbul and Cambridge stelae seems originally to have been as much painterly as sculptural. The earlier archaic grave stelae of East Greece tend to have tall, plain shafts with short incised inscriptions near the top and, often, palmette finials above.[3] Is it possible that in some of the main centres their plain shafts may originally also have carried painted scenes, executed either directly on the stone or on wooden panels, in a period coinciding with some of the highest attainments of Ionic art and thought, and was it in these that such new ideas first evolved? Possible confirmation for such a view might be derived from the readiness with which these stelae adopted relief decoration at a slightly later date, whether in a local East Greek, Atticizing or Graeco-Persian style. And is it that what we now have from Saqqâra and Chalcedon are local provincial versions of such paintings that have mercifully preserved the essentials of their composition because mixed techniques of sculpture and painting were used, instead of painting alone? This might also account for the rare re-emergence of such 'dialogue'-type compositions on Greek tombstones of the early fifth century B.C., notably on the Basle relief[4] and on a stela from Aegina which repeats the motif of the final clasping of hands.[5] Whatever the answer to the questions raised here, it will be seen that the Cambridge stela is a work of considerable iconographic importance.

[1] Cf. Austin, op. cit. 21–2; H. S. Smith, *A Visit to Ancient Egypt, Life at Memphis and Saqqara* (c. 500–30 B.C.) (Warminster, 1974), 43–5; also pp. vi–vii above.

[2] See pp. 75–9.

[3] D. C. Kurtz and J. Boardman, *Greek Burial Customs* (London, 1971), 221–2, 364 (where bibliography).

[4] E. Berger, *Das Basler Arztrelief* (Basle, 1970), *passim*, frontispiece, figs. 1, 8–21.

[5] Ibid. 111, fig. 132.

Additional Bibliography: *Cambridge Evening News*, 6 Apr. 1971, 5, with fig.; *Ann. Report Fitzwilliam Mus. Syndicate*, 1971, 9, pl. 1; *Gaz. des Beaux-Arts* 79 (1972), *Suppl.*, *Chron. des Arts*, p. 125, fig. 462.

4. H5–1343   Plates IV, 1; XXXIII, 1

This fine limestone stela, which was found in two halves in separate excavation seasons, is the most developed of a group of three, similar in subject-matter, found in the Sacred Animal Necropolis at Saqqâra.[1] It is divided horizontally into three registers, in the uppermost of which there is a winged disk with pendent uraei. The line of the primary and secondary feathering of the wings is shown, but the feathers themselves were not indicated by the sculptor. The wings do not, as is customary, follow the outline of the top of the stela, but the top breaks into the border which runs round the edge of the monument. Another unusual feature is the manner in which the artist has shown the junction of the uraei at the top of the disk, with their pointed tails revealed below.

In the scene below, the god Osiris is seen enthroned in the normal Egyptian fashion. The decorative design on the sides of the throne is an attempt to imitate the panel of diminishing squares which usually originate from the lower left-hand corner of the throne. Usually, the throne itself is mounted on a platform in the shape of the hieroglyphic sign for *ma'at*. In this instance, however, only the feet of Osiris are mounted, the sloping front of the sign being obscured by the column of the table laden with offerings in front of Osiris. The god wears the Upper Egyptian crown flanked by feathers, and in this representation is shown with horns, placed in a curious position, springing from the front of the right ear. The mummiform wrappings are open at the neck in a V-shape, and Osiris grasps the *was*- rather than the usual *ḥeḳat*-sceptre in his left hand,[2] and the flail in his right, the hands emerging from the wrappings in a strange manner. The flail is rendered in a very inexpert way.

Behind Osiris, and standing with her feet slightly apart, is a goddess wearing the vulture headdress supporting a diadem from which emerge the horns and disk. The top of the latter disappears into the curved outline of the pendent wing in the lunette of the stela. The wings of the goddess —who must from many parallels be identified with Isis—enfold Osiris in a protective embrace. No attempt has been made in this register or in those beneath to render the details of the faces.

The stela-owner advances from the right, his hands raised in the gesture of adoration. His kilt is abnormally short. One arm touches the stems of an open lotus flower and bloom, which together with four round loaves and two trussed ducks (very summarily shown) form the offering on the altar before the god. The altar itself is un-Egyptian in type, consisting simply of a straight vertical post without a base, supporting a flat table.

A horizontal band separates the upper from the middle register, and is incised with a Carian inscription, which continues down the right-hand margin of the stela (see p. 23 above).

In the second register, the ibis-headed god of wisdom, Thoth, is shown on the right, his hands raised in adoration of an image of the Apis Bull. Thoth wears the usual tripartite wig. His kilt, however, is curiously short, and the front fold and bottom hem are drawn in an un-Egyptian fashion. But even more bizarre is Thoth's posture, with knees bent and rear heel raised, the body being held in a semi-crouching position of obeisance foreign to Egyptian art, and normally unthinkable for an Egyptian deity. Before the god is an offering-table of the type shown in the register above, upon which are placed two open lotus flowers and a bud.

[1] Cf. **5, 5a.**   [2] Cf. **5, 6.**

The conventional iconography of the Apis bull is clearly shown on this stela. Between his horns he bears the disk with uraeus, shown emerging in the latter case from the disk and not placed, as is usual, on the bull's brow. The cloth over his back—decorated in many representations—is flanked by the wings of vultures. There is a clearly defined tuft at the end of the bull's tail and the animal is, on the whole, well drawn according to the Egyptian canon.

The goddess Isis stands behind the Apis in a position of protection. Iconographically, she is indistinguishable from the representation above, except that the feather of *maᶜat*, 'Truth', is held aloft in her left hand and that the details of the feathering, executed in red painted lines, are preserved on the lower wing. The head-dress of the goddess cuts through the border dividing the two registers, a solecism that would not normally be tolerated in an Egyptian atelier.

The lowest register, which is divided from the middle by a plain border, bears a scene of extraordinary interest, entirely un-Egyptian in character and only rarely depicted in Egyptian sources. It shows a dead woman, possibly the wife or a relative of the worshipper in the upper register, lying on an elaborate bier with a table of food beside it. The iconography of this remarkable scene, which also includes male and female mourners grieving for the dead woman and supporting her head, is quite un-Egyptian and is discussed in detail below by Mr. Nicholls. Traditional Egyptian scenes showing female mourners have been collected by Werbrouck.[1] Representations of the deceased as a mummy on a bier, with attendant priests and others, are commonplace in ancient Egyptian mourning scenes on reliefs, paintings, and funerary papyri. But the corpse is rarely depicted clothed in the apparel of daily life, although one notable exception may be cited in a relief scene dating from the later Eighteenth Dynasty.[2] The reluctance of artists in the ancient Near East to depict the unembalmed dead body, other than, for example, in battle scenes, is worthy of remark and would repay further investigation.

Before proceeding to a detailed description of its bottom register, it seems desirable to stress that the whole stela was clearly carved by the same hand, with the possible exception of the inscription. Thus the worshipper and human-headed Egyptian deities in the upper two registers carry the same distinctive faces, in a provincial East Greek style, as the corpse and mourners in the bottom scene where the idiom is local Greek throughout. The Carian inscription does not establish beyond doubt that the artist was Carian-speaking, although this is quite likely. It seems to have been fitted in a little clumsily after the carving had been completed and thus might have been added by a second craftsman. But whether the artist was a Caromemphite or a Hellenomemphite, his native style was a distinctive local provincial East Greek, and he was also clearly thoroughly steeped in Egyptian art and Egyptian traditions. The important thing to stress is probably not so much his occasional departures from Egyptian conventions in the top two registers of the stela as that a wholly alien artist came so close to adopting these conventions in all other respects. In the bottom scene he lapses into his native idiom. Such stelae from Memphite workshops in a local archaic East Greek style have been discussed as a whole above.[3] In the present case, the juxtaposition of the Greek and Egyptian elements reveals how much the incised technique of the stelae from these workshops owed to that of Egyptian shallow sunk relief-work in the way it faintly suggests the modelling of the figures. Even so, as one passes into a more truly Greek idiom in the bottom register, rather more use tends to be made of plain incised drawing of the Greek kind, particularly for rendering detail. The

[1] M. Werbrouck, *Les pleureuses dans l'Égypte ancienne* (Brussels, 1938), *passim*.

[2] W. Spiegelberg, *Ausgewählte Kunstdenkmäler* (Strass-burg, 1909), pl. 8; Werbrouck, op. cit., pl. 16; M. Guentch-Ogloueff-Doresse in *RdE* 4 (1940), 75–80.

[3] Pp. 64–8 above.

lower part of the stela is also notable for the way that it preserves traces of the red pigment in which parts of it were painted. The other colours have now vanished, apart from extremely faint traces of yellow and some meagre indications that large, full-face eyes, apparently with black outlines and central pupils, were once painted on the profile faces of the figures. The small scale doubtless also limited the amount of detail that could be shown, whether by painting or incision, since the maximum height of the frame bounding the bottom register is only 16·1 cm.

The bottom scene shows the laying out, or *prothesis*, of a dead woman. She is of matronly, indeed statuesque proportions and is shown lying on her back on a couch with her arms at her sides. Painted red lines seem to have been used to indicate the fingers of her left hand in much the same way as red linear detail is employed to show the feathers of Isis' wing in the middle register of the stela. The dead woman appears to be wearing a sleeved *chiton*, possibly originally painted yellow. Her feet are also swathed in cloth and it is possible that, if the long *chiton* was not tucked up at the waist, its surplus length may well have served to wrap the feet. The middle part of her *chiton* is, in fact, hidden by a small pall, which extends from below her breasts to above her ankles. It is draped over her body, but leaves her arms free, and the way that it hangs suggests that weights may have been stitched into its four corners. Such rather meagre palls are a distinctive feature of the *prothesis* scenes on the Memphite stelae and will be discussed further below.

The dead woman is also decked out in her jewellery. She has two plain bracelets on her left arm and a broad band above her brow, confining her red hair and tucked in under the main locks hanging down at the back. As this seems to have been a short band without long hanging ends, it is probably not a fillet but a funerary diadem of a kind that long remained popular and that has been found in actual burials, fashioned of thin gold sheet.[1] In her ears she wears W-shaped ear-rings of a kind especially popular in East Greece and the Aegean islands.[2] They had developed in the seventh century B.C. and persisted on through the fifth century B.C.; those on the corpse seem to show the pyramidal tips of the rather more evolved examples. Around her neck the dead woman has a double necklet of spherical beads, to which is attached a pendant in the form of a head of a bull or cow. Bull's head pendants are soundly attested in East Greek and island gold jewellery of the seventh and fifth centuries B.C.[3] But in the present instance the length of neck associated with the head calls more to mind the East Greek scent bottles of the end of the seventh and the sixth centuries B.C. and other decorative *protomai*.[4] But, although this prominent amulet may well have been intended to be understood as of Greek workmanship, it is difficult not to associate its wearing with the protection of the bovine deities, Apis and Isis, his mother, shown in the scene immediately above and whose protection for the deceased the stela was presumably intended to invoke.

The corpse's head is supported on a pillow and the rest of her body by a thick red mattress. This mattress was originally represented as elaborately embroidered with Greek motifs, a key pattern above and a meander below, rendered in lines of colour applied over the red. This applied colour has flaked away and, in some places, it has taken the red with it, so that the outline of the pattern survives as a faint reserved line on the red. Such traces are now only clearly visible at the foot end

[1] R. A. Higgins, *Greek and Roman Jewellery* (London, 1961), 121–2.

[2] Ibid. 106–8 types 2–3, 115 types 2–3, 123–4 type 2, fig. 17, pls. 17 *b–d*, 21*d*, 22*d*, 24*f*, 25 *c, f*.

[3] F. H. Marshall, *BMC Greek, Etruscan and Roman Jewellery* (London, 1911), 99 no. 1198, pl. 12; Higgins, op.

cit. 110, 127, pl. 26.

[4] J. Ducat, *Les Vases plastiques rhodiens* (Paris, 1966), 102–6, pls. 3, 14. Later gold bull's-head pendant of just this form: A. Greifenhagen, *Schmuckarbeiten in Edelmetall, Antikenabteilung, Berlin*, i (Berlin, 1970), 42, pl. 19. 6–7.

of the couch, but other faint indications seem to confirm that originally both patterns extended the full length of the mattress.

The couch on which the corpse lies is of a distinctive variety with round, possibly lathe-turned legs. Although this may have had remote antecedents in Egypt,[1] the present representation is of a type of couch that is unmistakably Greek, and at a stage in its development that evolved in Greece in late archaic times.[2] The artist has been at pains to suggest how the different components were joined together. In particular, he stresses the way in which the sides of the couch were mortised through the turned legs. He also seems to show locking pegs securing the tenons from above. These may actually also be the tenons fastening the ends of the couch. Certainly, the corner-bosses at the tops of the legs are exceptionally high on the present couch and this might have been done to accommodate the couch ends set at this higher level.

Around the couch stand four mourners, two women and two beardless and possibly youthful men with long hair. The heads of all these figures are allowed to extend above the line framing the top of the scene. With the possible exception of one of the women, who is more simply dressed and may be intended as a servant or a professional mourner, they probably represent the children or other close relatives of the dead woman. At the head of the couch, a lady with her long hair hanging loose down her back, is engaged in adjusting the head of the corpse on its pillow. There are faint traces of displaced yellow pigment on the lady's dress and on the background in its vicinity, although which surface it originally came from is no longer clear. The dress itself is a very long sleeved *chiton* with the surplus material tucked up over the girdle in front to form a deep *kolpos*, so that the hem clears the feet although it trails on the ground behind in a sort of train. This special development from the Ionic *chiton* seems to have been the normal dress of Caromemphite women in archaic times.[3] It seems to have been evolved locally. The normal dress of Carian women was the Ionic *chiton* which, indeed, Herodotus regarded as having originated in Caria.[4] But in Caria they seem to have worn it according to existing Ionian fashions, to judge from archaic East Greek sculptures found in Caria and, rather more relevantly, from the local terracottas, once these began to render costume realistically in advanced late archaic times.[5] The other woman faces the lady just described from behind the bier. She has red hair and appears to be tearing her cheek in lamentation. She is dressed in a simpler, shorter *chiton* of similarly opaque linen which terminates above her ankles, and which is apparently worn without a *kolpos*.[6] It has already been suggested that this difference in dress may indicate a difference in status and that the woman tearing her cheek may be a servant or a professional mourner.[7]

The two men approach the far side of the bier just behind this woman. Each is dressed in a *chiton* of thin, virtually transparent, linen which extends down to the lower calves.[8] The leading man holds a curious, curved implement in front of his face. Its shape somewhat recalls the contemporary Greek single-edged slashing sword, the *machaira* or *kopis*, if this were held with its cutting edge towards the man's face and brow.[9] One is reminded of Herodotus' account of the way that the

---

[1] G. M. A. Richter, *Furniture of the Greeks, Etruscans and Romans* (2nd ed., London, 1966), 55, fig. 292; but compare the much later Greek-influenced bed from Thebes, ibid. 56, fig. 298.

[2] Ibid. 55–8, figs. 293–7, 299–308; Kyrieleis, *Throne und Klinen*, 116–51, pl. 17.

[3] Cf. pp. 62, 64, 81–2, 84–5.

[4] v, 88.

[5] e.g. Pryce, *BMC Greek and Roman Sculpture*, i, Part 1, 149–50 no. B 319, fig. 188; Richter, *Korai*, 93 no. 167, figs. 532–5. For the late archaic terracottas, see especially R. A. Higgins, *BMC Greek Terracottas*, i (London, 1954), 106–10 nos. 324–43, pls. 51–2.

[6] A fault-line in the stone gives a false appearance of an incised line towards the front of the garment under the couch; actually it is quite plain.

[7] Cf. p. 85 for a similar figure.

[8] Cf. pp. 62, 64 above.

[9] Cf. A. M. Snodgrass, *Arms and Armour of the Greeks* (New York, 1967), 97–8, pl. 50.

Carians living in Egypt mutilated their own brows with this weapon as a gesture of ritual mourning.[1] Precisely the same implement appears in the right hand of the leading male mourner on the Abûsîr stela, but there it is shown distinctly thinner and so looks less like a lethal weapon.[2] Zahn has interpreted it as a kind of fly-whisk, an implement that it was also useful to have to hand during a *prothesis*, and in this he may equally be right. Until further examples come to light to clarify the matter, all that can be said is that the same interpretation must apply for both stelae. The second man is red-haired and has his hands raised to his head in lamentation.

Beside the couch, partly concealing the legs of the last three mourners, stands a three-legged table with a red top, spread with ritual food. Tables of this form may also have had much earlier Egyptian and Palestinian antecedents in the second millennium B.C.,[3] but the present representation is of an unmistakably Greek variety.[4] Its two legs at the projecting end are of a rectangular shape with incised lines at the top and bottom, probably indicating plain mouldings. Its single leg at the other end terminates in an animal-claw foot. A horizontal stretcher member links this leg with the stretcher between the other two legs and concealed behind them. Above this stretcher, the back of the single, animal-claw leg is decorated with a volute and a half-palmette.[5] In the space between the stretcher and the top of the table there are fretted vertical struts in the form of volutes and buds.[6] Alternating with these struts and apparently resting on the stretcher are inverted lotus blossoms and at either end there are small round objects, one against the half-palmette and two between the rectangular legs. It is not clear how far this narrow stretcher member on Greek portable tables also served to carry small items of food, etc.[7] But scenes showing similar small roundels above the stretcher on tables being tipped to be carried would seem to indicate that these, and probably also the inverted lotus blossoms in the present representation, are part of the fretted decoration and not actual berries, etc., placed on the stretcher.[8] In that case the lotus flowers are inverted to provide a suitable alternation with the volute-and-bud decoration.

The table's red top carries various items of Greek ritual food. At each end there is a pair of pyramidal cakes, or *pyramides*.[9] In view of the uncertainties surrounding the derivation of the word, pyramid, itself, the circumstance that these early and extremely clear representations are from Egypt is at least of passing interest. The object next to the left pair of pyramidal cakes appears to be a *popanon*, a kind of flat cake used for offerings. Next to the two right-hand *pyramides* are a pair of pomegranates. And in the centre of the table, between the pomegranates and the *popanon*, there is an irregularly shaped object of more or less oval form. The artist seems to have intended a loaf of bread, but it is difficult to explain the two tiny incised strokes on the edge of his oval. Apart from the bread, these offerings have rather narrow and specific cult implications. To judge from Greek votive reliefs, the combination of *pyramides* and *popana* is peculiar to the ritual feasts offered to certain chthonic and fertility deities and to the much more widely attested symbolic banquets offered heroes or the 'blessed' dead—that is to say, the dead who were regarded as having achieved

[1] ii, 61.

[2] p. 64 above, no. A2, p. 91, pl. XXX.

[3] Baker, *Furniture*, 153, 224, figs. 237, 358.

[4] Richter, *Furniture*, 66–9, figs. 286, 290, 294, 296–7, 299, 311–17, 331–2, 342–58.

[5] A fault-line in the stone falsifies the appearance of the lower petal of the palmette, making it wrongly seem at first to have been cut off short as if its tip was a second roundel.

[6] For such decorative struts on tables see Richter, op. cit.,

figs. 296, 593; Kyrieleis, op. cit., pl. 16.1. For the disjunctive character of the ornament, compare the fretted decoration above the stretcher of a couch on a *hydria* by the Berlin Painter, Richter, op. cit., fig. 321.

[7] Cf. Richter, op. cit., 67.

[8] e.g. ibid., fig. 343.

[9] For the derivation of πυραμίς, cf. πυραμοῦς. The pyramids are often regarded as having acquired their Greek name from their resemblance in shape to these cakes.

a kind of part-divine immortality. The pomegranates are closely associated with Persephone and other chthonic deities and also with the cult of the dead. The table and its offerings introduce a quite new feature into the iconography of the Greek *prothesis* and their significance will be discussed further below.

It now remains to consider the date of the British Museum stela. The flat treatment of the drapery in the *prothesis* scene and the style of the heads both still seem to echo East Greek work of the third quarter of the sixth century B.C., if not very clearly or specifically. The dead woman's finery unfortunately affords only a very approximate guide as to date, because of the dearth of finds of Greek jewellery from the sixth century B.C. The furniture in the *prothesis* scene is much more helpful, in particular the couch. Turned legs of the form that it shows are already adumbrated in the late third quarter of the sixth century B.C. on some of the backless thrones, or *diphroi*, of the deities on the frieze of the Siphnian Treasury at Delphi.[1] To judge from representations, couches of the present form were widespread in the last quarter of the sixth century B.C. and continued on into the fifth century B.C.[2] A date earlier than the last quarter of the sixth century B.C. would thus seem unlikely for the British Museum stela. It may, nevertheless, have been produced quite early in the last quarter of the century. First of all, despite the quite considerable differences in style and proportions, it still shows remarkable correspondences in composition and iconography with the Abûsîr stela, which has been tentatively dated above to the later third quarter of the sixth century B.C.[3] Also, it seems distinctly earlier in style than the other two stelae of Group B which, as will be seen below, are the work of a single artist, the Saqqâra Master.[4] Yet, both of the Saqqâra Master's stelae would seem to date before the end of the sixth century B.C.

Other Memphite stelae show closely similar *prothesis* scenes—the Abûsîr example in Berlin cited above and the two others by the Saqqâra Master also mentioned above and published in this volume, in addition to the British Museum stela now under discussion. To these may be added a fifth Memphite stela, also in Berlin, showing the *prothesis* of a 'Mede' in a Graeco-Persian style.[5] On the tentative chronology advanced in this study, all five would seem to have been produced in about the last third of the sixth century B.C.

The *prothesis* normally occupied the second day of a Greek funeral and consisted of the laying out of the corpse on a couch, apparently in the courtyard of the house, and the lamentation of the family.[6] In Greek art of the sixth century B.C. the practice is abundantly portrayed in Athens, mainly on painted vases and terracotta funerary plaques.[7] Indeed, it had been a popular theme for Attic vase-painters since the mid eighth century B.C. Elsewhere in the Greek world isolated representations confirm the widespread adoption of the practice, but there is little to rival the rich visual documentation of the Attic scenes. Local practices in this respect are very poorly attested in East Greek art and it is against this background that the series of five Memphite *prothesis* scenes constitutes, in itself, a both rich and important body of evidence, although it is at this stage by no means clear how far the local usages they reveal are broadly East Greek or narrowly Caromemphite. Indirectly of interest, also, are the *prothesis* reliefs on several of the Etruscan funerary *cippi*

---

[1] Kyrieleis, op. cit. 123, 131, 134, pls. 17.1, 24.1.

[2] Cf. the surviving early-fifth-century-B.C. couch of this type from Duvanli, ibid. 126–9, pl. 17.3–4.

[3] p. 64–5 above, no. A2, pl. XXX.

[4] See p. 82 below. These are **5**, stela with *prothesis* of woman, and **5a**, stela with *prothesis* of man. On Group B and its dating see also p. 65–6 above.

[5] p. 66 above, no. C1.

[6] Kurtz and Boardman, *Burial Customs*, 143–4.

[7] W. Zschietzschmann, 'Die Darstellungen der Prothesis in der griechischen Kunst' in *Ath. Mitt.* 53 (1928), 17–47, Beil. 8–18; J. Boardman, 'Painted Funerary Plaques and some Remarks on Prothesis' in *BSA* 50 (1955), 51–66, pls. 1–8.

from Chiusi, the ancient Clusium.[1] These reliefs seem to have been inspired by the scenes on the Attic plaques and vases, but the East Greek traits in the local late archaic Etruscan style in which they are executed may occasionally seem to bring them closer to the Memphite stelae than is actually the case.

In general, the Memphite *prothesis* scenes accord very closely with the Greek examples from Athens and elsewhere. The corpse lies on a couch spread with a thick mattress (or three in the case of the Graeco-Persian relief) and with a pillow under its head. On the Abûsîr stela and on the Saqqâra Master's *prothesis* of a man the couch is of the Greek rectangular-legged variety with a narrow section flanked by volutes part way down, whereas on the British Museum stela and on the Saqqâra Master's other example it is of a Greek type with turned legs. On both of the Saqqâra Master's stelae the couch legs rest in turn on exceptionally spreading volute stands. Plainer leg-stands are in evidence on the Abûsîr stela and the Graeco-Persian relief. On the Graeco-Persian relief, however, the couch is appropriately of a Near Eastern instead of a Greek variety. On this relief the corpse is that of a richly bearded 'Median' male and on one of the Saqqâra Master's stelae it appears to be that of a beardless man with a *sakkos* wound round his head in a kind of turban. On the Saqqâra Master's other example and on the British Museum stela the corpse is that of a fully dressed woman. On the Abûsîr stela, where some of the mistaken attempts to reconstruct the inscription have implied that the deceased was female, the hair treatment might seem appropriate, but not the bare feet and the absence of developed breasts. There is a possible solution to this problem. It is noteworthy that on all the other four stelae the corpse is shown on a larger scale than the mourners, as befitting its greater importance. On the Abûsîr stela, however, the dead body is actually somewhat smaller than any of the other figures. It is thus possible that, in this case, the artist may have intended to portray not an adult, but a child, possibly a boy, lying on the bier. The Graeco-Persian relief shows a drape hanging over the side of the couch and a sort of canopy behind and above the corpse. On all the other four stelae the dead body is draped from just above or below the breast to a little above the ankles in a rather meagre pall whose four corners hang steeply down and would seem to have had weights sewn into them. The arms of the corpse are placed above this pall and so fully exposed. The meagreness of this pall is in sharp contrast to the close swathing of most of the body, apart from the head, usual in the Attic and other *prothesis* scenes.

To turn now to the mourners, the important position at the head of the couch, adjusting the head of the corpse on its pillow, is in all cases occupied by a woman, as is also the rule on the Attic examples. On the Saqqâra Master's stelae all of the mourners are women. On the others both men and women are present, but the men occupy a position near the foot of the couch, as also tends to be the case in the Attic scenes. A similar curved object is held by the leading male mourner on both the Abûsîr and British Museum stelae but, as has been seen above, it is not yet adequately determined whether this is a weapon for self-mutilation or a fly-swat. On the British Museum stela and the Saqqâra Master's *prothesis* of a man one of the women mourners seems to wear a much simpler kind of *chiton*, and it has been suggested above that she may be either a servant or a professional mourner. As might be expected, oddities of dress also occur on the Graeco-Persian relief, where the women mourners are bare-breasted and the men, apart from the groom, who may have been Egyptian, are in 'Median' dress.

[1] G. Q. Giglioli, *L'arte etrusca* (Milan, 1935), xxxii–xxxiii, pls. 138.1, 143.1, 144.2, 146, 147; E. Paribeni 'I rilievi chiusini arcaici' in *St. etruschi* 12 (1938), 57–139 especially pls. 7.1, 21.1–2, 22.1, 23.1, 24.1, 25.2–3, 32.1–2; id. in *St. etruschi* 13 (1939), 179–202.

Certain of the Memphite *prothesis* scenes show a completely unusual feature. On the Abûsîr, British Museum, and Graeco-Persian stelae there is a table placed beside the couch. On the Graeco-Persian relief this table is also of a Near Eastern type, but on the others it is an ordinary Greek three-legged table. In the original publication of the Abûsîr stela Zahn has already remarked that the presence of the table seemed to suggest a link between what was otherwise a moderately conventional *prothesis* scene and the Greek funerary banquet reliefs—a natural enough assumption since couch and table would only normally be combined for purposes of banqueting and the table is placed beside the bier as though it is the corpse that has feasted.[1] Zahn assumed that the conflation of the *prothesis* with the funerary banquet was due to an error on the part of the artist, but the combined testimony of the three stelae makes it reasonably certain that local funerary practices in some way linked the *prothesis* with some form of symbolic meal.

The Greek funerary banquet reliefs show a kind of ritual feast set, to judge from their all too infrequent inscriptions, occasionally before chthonic deities but more usually before heroes, themselves the great dead of long ago raised to the level of demi-gods, and then only gradually, and not frequently until Hellenistic times, before ordinary dead mortals shown in a 'heroized' or quasi-deified state.[2] These reliefs also begin in the later sixth century B.C., initially as a rather special and stereotyped kind of banqueting scene, but the distinctive attributes, the special drinking vessels, the ritual food on the table, and the divine *polos* on the head of the principal figure, all these only emerge at much later stages. There seems to be some kind of direct link between the Saqqâra *prothesis* scenes and probably not so much the incipient funerary banquet reliefs themselves as the already existing beliefs and ideas that they were later to be adapted to convey. This is strongly suggested by the ritual food set out on the table on the British Museum relief, especially the *pyramides* and *popanon* which were later to become the special fare of the heroes and 'blessed' dead, as represented on the funerary banquet reliefs. Thus the Memphite stelae would seem to open a new chapter in ancient funerary beliefs and practices. For it is obvious that the banquet involved is of a purely ritual kind and quite different from the great feast, the *perideipnon*, that took place after the funeral was over.[3] It is also of interest to note that the table is empty on the Abûsîr and Graeco-Persian stelae, as if these represent a stage when this symbolic banquet had just been completed. For, in accordance with Greek custom, one would expect the portable table to have been carried in already laid with food. Who, then, took part in this ritual meal? Was it simply the close relatives at the time of the *prothesis* or has there been a conflation in time in some of these scenes and was the sacred food offered earlier on the deathbed, when the dying person was still alive, as bringing a promise of immortality?[4] The latter interpretation might more readily account for the circumstance that on two of the stelae the table is already empty and on two others it would seem to have been already removed. The last two examples, lacking the table, are the Saqqâra Master's stelae and both may show the same stage in the *prothesis*, the lament of the women.

Thus the ritual banquet may itself also imply a much more positive attitude towards the after-life and towards the immortality of the dead and their status in the hereafter. The Egyptian influences that permeated the lives of this Memphite community may have played a part in all this—one has only to remember how the top registers of all the *prothesis* stelae of Group B show a member

---

[1] R. Zahn in Borchardt, *Grabdenkmal des Königs S'aḥu-reꜤ*, i, 137.

[2] R. N. Thönges-Stringaris, 'Das griechische Totenmahl' in *Ath. Mitt.* 80 (1965), 1–99, Beil. 1–30; for the early examples, ibid. 3–13; for their significance, ibid. 58–68.

[3] Kurtz and Boardman, *Burial Customs*, 146.

[4] Is it not possible that the strange symbolism of the funerary banquet reliefs is as much to be accounted for by some such simple mystic ceremony as by the prospect of uninterrupted dining rights in the hereafter?

of the same family making offerings to Isis and Osiris. But sixth-century-B.C. art in Greece itself already shows the stirrings of new attitudes towards the dead even before the earliest of the funerary banquet reliefs. One might instance the grave statues with their elusive cult implications, the terracotta *poloi* placed in some Boeotian graves, and the Laconian reliefs apparently showing heroes or 'heroized' dead receiving offerings.[1] Here we shall limit ourselves to drawing attention to one monument which brings us back to the main theme of the *prothesis*. This is one of the earliest of the Attic *prothesis* plaques and it shows the corpse of a woman wearing a divine *polos* on its head.[2] This evidence is purely visual and so does not make it clear what kind of mystery beliefs lay behind these developments. But it does at least suggest that these curious features occurring on the Memphite stelae may at least be in part due to remarkable changes taking place in Greece itself. Plato implies that it was Orphism that opened the way to a festive eternity, possibly of the kind depicted on the funerary banquet reliefs,[3] but other mystery beliefs may have been an even more potent and more spiritual force in this. One has only to recall how the *pyramides* and *popana* are also represented as offered to Demeter and Persephone and alluded to as the contents of the sacred *cista* of their mysteries and how the *cista* itself seems occasionally to appear on funerary banquet reliefs, even those from East Greece.[4]

But how does all this relate to the Egyptian scenes of the upper registers of the British Museum stela and of the other examples of Group B and what did these mean to the members of the foreign communities who actually set them up? The top register shows a man making offerings to the god, Osiris, and the goddess, Isis, divinities whom the early Greek settlers in Egypt equated with their own deities, Dionysos and Demeter.[5] The conventions of Egyptian funerary stelae would suggest that the man is a close member of the same family who is celebrated by the scene as already dead and in the actual presence of the immortals and not, on the analogy of Greek scenes, the dedicant of the stela worshipping at a temple. In the second register the offerings are made instead by a divine proxy and one singularly eloquent and apt both for the cult of the dead and that of Isis and Osiris, Thoth, whom the Greeks in Egypt interpreted as their own god, Hermes.[6] He is making offerings to the Apis bull and, again, to Isis-Demeter, doubtless here in the guise of Isis, Mother-of-Apis. Apis occupies precisely the position in the second register that Osiris fills in the upper, both shielded by Isis' wings. Sacred cow burials of the Mothers-of-Apis in the vicinity of the temple near which these stelae were found are recorded on Egyptian stelae from the area as far back as the time of Amasis, although the Iseum in use prior to the fourth century B.C. has possibly still to be found.[7] There is thus a distinct local aptness in these scenes. The recurrent figure in the upper registers is Isis, the Demeter of the Greeks, and both the scenes might indeed be connected with those mysteries of Isis that were to take such a hold on the Greek mind. It is probably this same Isis-Demeter who reappears later as the sceptred goddess on a Greek painted *pinax* also from Saqqâra.[8]

If the upper registers suggest the promise of immortality made by the cults of Isis and Osiris,

[1] For general bibliography on these and related topics, see Kurtz and Boardman, op. cit., *passim*. In some areas the placing of terracotta statuettes of banqueters in graves may be linked with the emergence of the funerary banquet reliefs; so, too, may the rare stelae, such as the example from Kos, with erotic banquet scenes.

[2] G. M. A. Richter, 'Terracotta Plaques from Early Attic Tombs' in *Bull. MMA* i (1942), 80–92, figs. 4, 6; id., *Archaic Greek Art* (Oxford, 1949), 8, fig. 8; id. *Handbook of Greek Collection, Met. Mus.* (Cambridge, Mass., 1953), 40, pl. 26*f*; id. *Furniture*, 58 f., fig. 309.

[3] *Republic* 363 c.

[4] Thönges-Stringaris, op. cit. 63, Beil. 14.2, 15.1.

[5] Herodotus ii, 42, 59.

[6] Note how a human participant is substituted on stela **6**.

[7] *JEA* 57 (1971), 1, 11–12; H. S. Smith, 'Dates of the Obsequies of the Mothers of Apis', *Rev. d'Ég.* 24 (1972), 176–87; *JEA* 59 (1973), 5–6; Smith, *Visit to Ancient Egypt*, 37–41.

[8] G. T. Martin in *JEA* 59 (1973), 13, pl. 14. Now British Museum, Greek and Roman Dept., inv. no. 1975.7–28.1; recently cleaned.

the bottom one reveals the harsh realities of death. But has there not been even here some direct conflation between the mysteries of Isis and those of Demeter, both proffering happiness in a life beyond death? Is the symbolic mystic banquet with its promise of immortality not possibly itself linked with the mysteries of Demeter, and so, of Isis? If self-mutilation is in fact being practised, as, it is suggested above, may possibly be the case, is this not the custom directly linked with Carian participation in the mysteries of Isis-Demeter at Busiris? May not even the amulet worn by the corpse be intended to claim the protection of that bovine aspect of Isis-Demeter worshipped at this spot that the early Greeks in Egypt linked also with Io and that so fascinated Herodotus?[1] As has been seen above, it might in that case quite well be associated with the Isis of the middle register.

The questions thus raised by these stelae are not yet all capable of being answered, but would seem to have considerable significance for the development of religious beliefs in the sixth century B.C.

5. H5–1228   Plates V, 1; XXXIII, 2

The second stela of the group is similar in many respects to **4**, but there are variations in detail. Again, the stela is divided into three registers by horizontal bands, the lower of which bears an incised Carian text, which continues upward into the middle register along the right-hand margin of the stela (see pp. 23–4 above).

In the lunette of the upper register there is a winged sun-disk with pendent uraei, the latter having ʿankh-signs suspended from their 'necks'. The pronounced incised dot in the centre of the sun-disk is noteworthy, and occurs elsewhere on the stela.[2] The symbol is obviously compass-drawn. The wings in the lunette are somewhat extended, and the tips break through the border of the stela, which is marked by an incised line.

Below, the owner of the stela is shown to the right, kneeling on his right knee, with arms raised in the traditional worshipping posture. The outlines of a collar are evident around his neck. The outline of the right leg is shown in front of the kilt. The right arm is concealed behind the body. No detail of the face of this figure or of the others on the same stela is indicated.

In front of the worshipper is a tall conical altar of normal Egyptian type, bearing offerings. The curved element at the left is probably to be interpreted as part of a trussed duck. Three open lotus blossoms on long stems are shown above.

Behind the offering-table the god Osiris is shown enthroned, garbed in the customary mummiform wrappings. The throne with recessed panelling designs on the side is of the normal Egyptian type, and here stands on the base-line. The cushion or cloth at the back is clumsily drawn. The footstool, the front of which is obscured by the left foot of the stela-owner, is probably in the form of the sign maʿat. Osiris wears the White Crown with flanking plumes, horns (springing over the ear) and long ceremonial beard, the latter following the curve of the cheek and ending in a point reminiscent of Greek or Etruscan work, and unfamiliar on representations of Egyptian deities. The back of the head is indicated by a straight line, with a streamer or counterpoise below, here roughly drawn, and sometimes seen on statues of Osiris in the round. The insignia carried by the god are carved in an un-Egyptian manner. The sceptre, held in the left hand, is not of the normal ḥeka(t)-type. The top is somewhat damaged, but was probably meant to represent a was,[3] the staff normally

---

[1] Herodotus ii, 41.
[2] And on **5a**. It is also present in the lunette of an other-   wise blank and unregistered limestone stela from the same location as **5a** and **6**.   [3] Cf. **4** and **6**.

carried by the Memphite deity Ptah. The bulbous terminal is highly unusual, and was doubtless wrongly carved for the forked or open-ended *was* (⌐). The flail is grasped in the right hand.

Behind Osiris stands the goddess Isis, holding an ʿankh-sign in her right hand, with her left arm raised in a protective gesture towards Osiris. There is nothing remarkable about the iconography of this figure, except that the compass-drawn sun-disk over her head is not supported by the usual horns and diadem. The sun's disk in this example obtrudes into the tip of the winged disk above. Three empty rectangles, which in a standard Egyptian stela would have contained the names of the deities and the stela-owner in hieroglyphs, have been incised by the sculptor. The label for the name of Osiris has been slightly displaced by the pendent uraeus, and was drawn by the craftsman over the lotus blooms.

In the middle register the god Thoth is seen at the right with his right arm raised in a gesture of greeting or adoration to the Apis Bull. Thoth wears his customary tripartite wig and stiff kilt. On his head he wears a disk, which in conventional iconography represents the moon and is usually supported by a crescent. Here, however, the sun-disk with central incised dot is drawn. In his left hand he holds an object probably intended to represent a scribal palette, or just possibly a papyrus roll containing one of his treatises on wisdom or magic. In front of the Apis stands a conical offering-table, piled with figs. The objects hanging at either side probably represent, in a schematic way, the necks of trussed ducks. Three open lotus blooms are shown above, the stems disappearing behind the kilt of Thoth.

The image of the Apis Bull stands on a plain plinth. The front in this instance is straight, though customarily it slopes in imitation of the hieroglyphic sign for *maʿat*. Apis wears the disk and horns, with a cloth over his back. The curved line on the flank to the right may represent the line of the leg, or is just possibly the remains of a roughly drawn vulture's wing.[1] The goddess Isis stands behind, apparently wearing the vulture head-dress, her wings as usual protecting the bull, and she holds aloft the emblem of 'Truth'. Her pendulous breast is shown in profile according to the Egyptian convention. The diadem, disk, and horns break through the margin into the register above. In the upper part of the scene are six upright column divisions, which in a normal Egyptian stela would have enclosed an hieroglyphic inscription.

The lowest register shows a scene of mourning, similar in character to that represented in **4**. It does not figure in the standard Egyptian repertory, and is thus dealt with in detail by R. V. Nicholls.

Again the bottom register shows the *prothesis*, or laying out, of a dead woman and once more the scene is rendered consistently in a provincial Greek style.[2] Again it seems clearly to be by the same artist as was responsible for the two upper registers of the stela where he has followed Egyptian themes and conventions as closely as his own different visual traditions would permit; in the bottom register he lapses back into his own natural idiom. Once again the Carian inscription is fitted in a little awkwardly, and quite probably was only added after the rest of the stela was complete.

In his excellent description of the upper registers, Dr. Martin has stressed the features that would seem puzzling to Egyptian eyes. Some of these departures from Egyptian conventions seem, however, accidental rather than deliberate. For drawing the sun and moon disks the artist seems to have

---

[1] As in **4** and **5a**.

[2] This stela and the next have remained in Egypt and the author has been unable to examine them at first hand. The descriptions given here are based on excellent photographs provided by Miss Anne Millard. Inevitably, uncertainty remains on some points of detail. The line drawings made at the time of excavation had been left incomplete; such detail as seemed quite certain has been added since, on the evidence of the photographs.

used an ordinary pair of Greek incising compasses, of the kind normally used for incising formal ornament such as bead-and-reel decoration on stone in readiness for painting. On the present stela he has pressed quite hard so that his incision of the circles was at least as deep as the rest of the cutting of the figures. The result has been that the centre point of the compasses has also dug a deep hole in the middle of the disks; whence the dot.

The bottom register is executed in shallow recessed relief, with limited use of supplementary incision. It seems quite well preserved, but much of the detail is very faint.[1] The dead woman lies on her back on a couch with her arms at her sides. She seems to be dressed in a sleeved *chiton* and her feet are also swathed in cloth, possibly, as suggested above for **4**, in the lower part of the same long linen *chiton* if this was worn without having the surplus material tucked up at the girdle.[2] Over the *chiton* she is draped with the usual rather meagre pall, apparently with weights sewn into its corners.[3] This extends from above her breast to her lower calves. Her arms lie above it and she wears a bracelet on her left wrist. A thick mattress supports her body and there is a pillow under her head. Her head seems to be wrapped in a head-cloth with its hemmed edge folded back over her brow, possibly a *sphendone* fastened underneath at the back of the head. Her long hair escapes from the bottom of it at the back, near the nape of the neck. To judge from the photographs, it is possible, but not certain, that a further lock of hair may have been brushed up over the head-cloth from behind the ear.

The couch on which the corpse lies is rather summarily rendered, but seems to have been of much the same type as that appearing on the British Museum stela,[4] with similar, possibly lathe-turned, legs and similar rather high corner bosses. It shows a marked difference, however, in the way that the legs themselves are mounted on broad stands in the form of double volutes. Such stands served not only to increase the height of the couch and with it the sense of importance of the occupant, but also to fulfil a useful structural role. Whereas Egyptian beds seem regularly to have allowed for some bending or movement in their frames, Greek couches seem to have been built as completely rigid pieces of furniture, in which any independent movement in frame or leg could weaken the whole structure. By providing fixed sockets each for a pair of legs, such stands would seem to have strengthened the whole couch, especially where they were themselves permanently anchored to the floor. In late archaic and classical times they seem to have been provided not so much for the present kind of Greek couch with turned legs, as for that with flat rectangular legs, and seem often to have been decorated with small volutes at the top.[5] Very similar in form to the stands on the present stela are those under a rectangular-legged couch in the Saqqâra *prothesis* of a man.[6] It is thus possible that this extremely spreading variety may have been a local Memphite speciality. Simpler stands appear in the Carian and 'Median' *prothesis* scenes on Memphite stelae in Berlin.[7]

The corpse is attended by four mourners, all of them women and all of them clad in what seems to emerge as the ordinary dress of Caromemphite ladies in this period—a long, opaque, sleeved *chiton*, trailing on the ground behind and worn with a large *kolpos* in front where the surplus material was tucked up over the girdle so that the hem cleared the feet.[8] The *kolpos* appears as a projection in front, extending down to a little above or below the knees. The lady at the head of the

---

[1] The less-clear details, such as eye treatment, have accordingly not been added on the drawing, pl. XXXIII, 2.

[2] p. 72 above.

[3] p. 76 above.

[4] pp. 73, 75 above.

[5] Richter, *Furniture*, figs. 312–23.

[6] No. **5a** below.

[7] p. 64 no. A2, and p. 66 no. C1; cf. p. 91.

[8] pp. 62, 73, 84–5.

couch has her left hand extended to the head of the corpse, which she is adjusting on its pillow, and her right hand bent back towards her right shoulder. Whether this gesture with her right hand is one of mourning or of reaching for the fastening of her *chiton* is not clear, but, as will be seen below, it is so characteristic of the artist involved as to become almost his signature. She has prominent breasts, partly hidden by her left arm, and a bracelet on her right wrist. Her long hair is bound together into a plait or 'club' behind her shoulders. The next mourner, standing facing her behind the bier, mirrors her gesture with her left hand raised to her left shoulder. Her right upper arm straddles the breast of the corpse, her right elbow being apparently concealed behind the dead woman's left arm, and her right hand is outstretched towards the corpse's chin. This is probably a gesture of love and affection.[1] But it may also have had the object of preventing the dead woman's jaw from dropping open—a problem which in some Greek *prothesis* scenes seems to have necessitated the use of a chin strap. The next woman behind her has her breast turned to the front, although her head remains in profile with her gaze directed at the face of the corpse. This woman has both her hands raised to her head in lamentation, in a gesture that brings this stela much closer than its Memphite predecessors to the traditions of the Attic *prothesis* scenes. The fourth mourner, by the foot of the couch, has turned her back on the dead woman and is seen wholly in profile. She seems to be making much the same demonstration of sorrow as her neighbour, with her hands raised to tear her hair. Below the couch, an incised line seems to separate the *kolpos* from the rest of her *chiton*. Faint indications on one of the photographs suggest the possibility that the two mourners at the head of the couch may have had their eyes rendered in a fashion familiar from earlier black-figure vase-painting—as a circle with a dot in the centre for the pupil, and with short lines out from the circle to either side near the bottom for the tear-duct and outer corner of the eye. If this could be confirmed as certain, a similar treatment might be postulated at least for the other figures in the bottom register; as befitting her more Egyptian character, the Isis in the second register seems to have had a leaf-shaped full-face eye in her profile head.

This stela has been assigned to Group B which is provisionally dated to the last quarter of the sixth century B.C.[2] As compared with the early Group B example, the British Museum stela,[3] the treatment of detail is much more summary, although the scale is much the same, and the style seems much freer and more advanced. Some details, such as the head-cloth and hair treatment of the corpse may help confirm a late-sixth-century date. The style is much more open to direct Greek influence, but still remains very conservative, especially in the way that it retains the old conventions for rendering the local Caromemphite and Hellenomemphite dress, which give the whole *prothesis* scene a very old-fashioned appearance.

With this stela a local artistic personality seems to emerge to whom other works can be related. We shall name him the Saqqâra Master. The following stelae seem to be connected with his work:

By the Saqqâra Master:
1. The present stela, **5**, pl. V, 1.
2. The stela no. **5a** below, pl. V, 2.

Near the Saqqâra Master:
1. Saqqâra, unregistered, p. 79 above, n. 2. (It sounds as if too little survives for it to be possible ever to confirm whether or not this stela is actually by the Saqqâra Master.)
2. The stela, no. **6** below, pl. IV, 2.

[1] Cf. the Cambridge stela, no. **3** above.　　　[2] Pp. 65–6 above.　　　[3] No. **4** above.

The Saqqâra Master is not a particularly original or careful artist, but his style is reasonably consistent. Many of his idiosyncracies have been touched on above. Of the stelae described as near him, no. **6** is quite close and probably from the same workshop, if not from the artist's own hand.

5a. H5–1223   Plates V, 2; XXXIV, 1

This stela is similar in spirit and execution to the two previously described, and like them is divided into three registers. The surface is much weatherworn[1] and some of the detail is lost. Apparently, the stela was never inscribed.

The lunette was originally filled with the customary disk and wings, of which only traces of the latter survive. Beneath, the stela-owner is shown kneeling in a gesture of adoration, facing a seated figure of the god Osiris. The left forearm is shown drawn across the chest. The long sweeping wing behind Osiris indicates that the goddess Isis originally stood there in her usual protective position. The remains of an offering-table with two lotus blooms and a trace of the stem of a third are seen in the centre. The empty rectangular labels would customarily have contained the names of Osiris and the deceased.

In the second register Thoth, originally holding an ʿankh-sign in his left hand, greets an image of the Apis Bull, standing on a rectangular base, and wearing his usual accoutrements. A concave offering-table with lotuses stands between. The other offerings, as in the scene above, have weathered away. Isis, as before, stands behind the bull, but only her wings, disk (with central dot), and legs remain. The labels are as usual empty. For reasons of space the label intended for Thoth has been placed behind him rather than in front of his head.

The remaining register depicts a funerary scene, the subject of a commentary by R. V. Nicholls.

There is little doubt that the three stelae, here **4**, **5**, and **5a**, were carved by foreign craftsmen, doubtless in a Memphite atelier. Two of the three scenes represented are based on common Egyptian prototypes, interpreted in a thoroughly non-Egyptian way.

Mercifully, the bottom register of this stela is much better preserved than the upper two registers. It shows the *prothesis*, or laying out, of a dead man, rendered in a local provincial Greek style.[2] As remarked above,[3] all three registers seem to be the work of the Saqqâra Master. What survives of the two upper scenes reveals his characteristic Egyptianizing style. It also shows his idiosyncracies, such as the rectangular recessed panels where Egyptian inscriptions seemed to be indicated, whether or not these were ever painted in on them, and the compass-drawn circles for the sun and moon disks. In the bottom register he reverts to his own natural provincial Greek idiom. Apparently, there is no trace of a Carian inscription. Either the stela was set up uninscribed or else, perhaps rather more probably, it had its foreign inscription painted on, to be completely obliterated in the subsequent weathering.

The bottom register is done partly in shallow sunk relief, especially marked at the heads of the figures, and partly in incised drawing, the latter technique being apparently used alone for some parts of the couch.[4] Relatively little detail seems to have been shown. The scale is much smaller

---

[1] Many of the stelae described in this commentary show considerable signs of weathering, showing that they had been exposed to the elements, presumably in the façades of tombs or as ex-votos in the vicinity of a temple, before they were reused in the Sacred Animal Necropolis.

[2] On the Memphite *prothesis* scenes and their significance see pp. 75–9.

[3] p. 82 above.

[4] This description and the completion of the drawing, pl. XXXIV, 1, based on photographs provided by Miss Anne Millard; see p. 80 n. 2.

than that of the other *prothesis* scenes, the maximum height of the incised frame bounding the bottom register being only 13.7 cm. This may in turn have imposed a greater reliance on the now vanished painted detail.

As usual, the dead man lies on his back on a couch, with his arms to his sides. He is apparently beardless and his shoulders, arms, and feet seem to be completely bare. From above his rather prominent chest to his lower calves his body is draped with the usual kind of pall met with in these Caromemphite *prothesis* scenes.[1] As usual, this leaves his arms free and seems to have had weights stitched into its corners. A remarkable feature is the broad band that it shows at its upper end, presumably originally in a contrasting colour. On his head the corpse wears a more or less conical cap. This is probably neither a metal helmet nor a felt *pilos*, but rather a long head-cloth, or *sakkos*, wrapped round and round to form a kind of conical turban. Such a head-dress has a long history in East Greece as worn by men for festive occasions, being especially prominent in Chiot vase-painting.[2] By the late sixth century B.C. this fashion had become very widespread throughout Greece and Etruria, although by this stage it was adopted by both men and women. A scene representing the *prothesis* of a man on a curious one-handled black-figure *kantharos* of the late sixth century B.C. shows the corpse wearing just such a turban.[3] On the present stela a faint incised line on the brow of the corpse below the turban may indicate the hair line. Otherwise, the hair seems to have been worn either cut short or gathered up into the turban.

The corpse is shown lying on its back on a thick mattress, with a pillow under its head. It is not clear whether or not the artist intended to indicate a further cushion or pillow under the dead man's buttocks and hands. The couch on which the mattress is spread is of a common Greek variety with flat, rectangular legs, each with a cut-out section flanked by volutes.[4] Amongst the Memphite *prothesis* scenes, such a couch is already attested on the Abûsîr stela.[5] On the present stela the volutes on the legs must originally have been touched in in paint, along with the palmettes between them, although the leg at the head end of the couch retains two incised lines that originally helped to pick out one of these palmettes. The sort of painted decoration involved is attested much later from Saqqâra on a throne-leg of rather similar type appearing on a painted *pinax*.[6] In the present scene, the projecting part at the top of the leg at the head end was probably also originally painted with volutes like those appearing on the Abûsîr stela. It is less clear whether similar decoration would have appeared on its counterpart at the foot end of the couch, where the leg is shown excessively high. The couch itself is one of those strengthened by having a stretcher member running parallel with the main frame.[7] This, obviously, was in front of the mourners standing behind the couch, as was doubtless once made clear by the painting, although it has accidentally been cut at two points by the incised outlines of their bodies. The legs of the couch themselves rest on spreading stands in the form of volutes and buds. It has been suggested that the stands of this particular shape may have been a local Graeco-Memphite development.[8] They seem also to have appealed to the Saqqâra Master.

The mourners attending the bier seem all to be women. Three of them have long hair and wear what seems to have been the normal dress of Caromemphite ladies, a very long, opaque sleeved

---

[1] See p. 76 above.

[2] e.g. E. R. Price in *JHS* 44 (1924), pls. V. 12–13, XI.

[3] Zschietzschmann in *Ath. Mitt.* 53 (1928), 31–2, 43 no. 89, Beil. 15; Boardman in *BSA* 50 (1955), 54 n. 21; Richter, *Furniture*, fig. 456.

[4] Richter, *Furniture*, 58–63, figs. 309–29; Kyrieleis, *Throne und Klinen*, 151–77, pls. 19–21.

[5] p. 64 above, no. A2, p. 91, pl. XXX.

[6] *JEA* 59 (1973), 13, pl. 14; now British Museum, Dept. of Greek and Roman Antiquities, inv. no. 1975.7-28.1.

[7] Richter, op. cit., figs. 321–2, 324–5; compare also the stretchers under the Greek tables discussed on p. 74 above.

[8] p. 81 above.

chiton, trailing on the ground behind, but worn with a large *kolpos* in front where the surplus material was hitched up over the girdle so that the hem cleared the feet.[1] The fourth woman, standing at the foot of the couch, is quite differently dressed. She wears a shorter *chiton* which terminates above her ankles, and which is apparently not tucked up at all at her waist. A similar figure appears on the British Museum stela, and it has been suggested that she may represent a servant woman or a professional mourner.[2] The present figure likewise seems to be tearing her cheeks in grief, but appears to wear her hair rather shorter. The lady standing at the head of the couch is considerably taller than the other two standing behind the couch, and might conceivably be intended as their mother. With her left hand she is adjusting the corpse's turbanned head on its pillow. Her right hand is bent back to her right shoulder in the Saqqâra Master's characteristic gesture and her hair is probably to be understood as being worn in much the same way as by the lady in the corresponding position in that artist's *prothesis* of a woman.[3] The present figure overlaps the outer line bounding the scene to the right, which shows through for the length of her body, but not at her head, which is more deeply cut. Her *kolpos* is shown as hanging down in front to about knee-level, as is also the case with the smaller lady shown facing her from behind the couch. The outline of the body of the yet smaller figure beside her behind the couch gives no clear indication of the length of the *kolpos*. This figure has turned her back on the corpse and is watching the woman tearing her cheek at the foot of the couch.

This stela has been assigned to Group B and, like the Saqqâra Master's *prothesis* of a woman, is probably to be dated to the late sixth century B.C., a date apparently partly confirmed by the turbanned head of the corpse.[4] It is a much less careful and less lively work than the artist's *prothesis* of a woman, but whether the awkward mannerisms that it shows, such as the ugly stylization of the feet in the *prothesis* scene, are a measure of slightly later date or greater haste is harder to determine.

6. H5–1222 Plates IV, 2; XXXIV, 2

This stela, which bears a Carian inscription (see pp. 24–5 above), is divided into two registers, both of which are incised with Egyptianizing scenes.

In the upper register the god Osiris is depicted seated on an undecorated throne with a low back, and with the outline of a cloth or cushion behind. It is mounted on a low plinth which was doubtless in the customary form of the Egyptian hieroglyph *maᶜat*, 'Truth' (⏥). In this instance, however, the front of the plinth is obscured by the foot of the worshipper at the right. Osiris wears the White Crown flanked by feathers, and is swathed in the usual mummiform wrappings. The hands protrude from the wrappings, the left grasping the flail and the right holding a sceptre. The latter appears to be a clumsy attempt to draw the *was* (𓌀) rather than the usual *ḥeḳa(t)* (𓋹).[5] A rough panel in front of the head of Osiris, empty save for a fortuitous scratch, would normally have borne the deity's name in hieroglyphs.

Behind Osiris stands a figure of a goddess with a sun-disk surmounting her tripartite wig. Her left arm is extended towards the back of the throne of Osiris (the fingers being very summarily drawn), the right arm being held vertically by the side according to the usual canon. An incised rectangle in front of her long, close-fitting dress would normally have shown her name in

---

[1] pp. 62, 64, 73, 81 above.
[2] No. **4** above.
[3] No. **5** above.

[4] Cf. pp. 65–6, 84.
[5] Cf. **4, 5.**

hieroglyphs. The goddess who by custom stands in this position behind Osiris, and who is obviously intended here, is Isis,[1] though iconographically her head-dress is unusual, since she should wear a diadem with the disk and cows' horns.

The stela-owner, wearing a long kilt, advances from the right, his hands raised in an attitude of adoration. Beneath his arms a lotus bloom is roughly carved. Flowers of this kind normally accompany other votive offerings laid on an altar.[2] Two lines, possibly accidental, or a mistake on the part of the craftsman, are carved at the left shoulder of the worshipper. A panel above his head would normally have served to designate his name and station in hieroglyphic.

The bottom register is divided from the upper by a band of lightly incised Carian inscription, which continues below in a vertical line at the top right-hand corner of the lower register. The scene in this register shows the stela-owner in a kneeling position, with one hand raised to worship an image of a bull-deity, the other held horizontally over the knee. From parallels in the present group of stelae,[3] and in many other Memphite sources, the bull is certainly the Apis, bearing the winged disk on his head. It is represented not as the living incarnation-animal but as a statue on a plinth, the latter very roughly drawn but intended to be in the form *maʿat* (see above).

Behind the Apis stands a figure of a goddess, with arms and wings outstretched in a protective embrace. Her head, surmounted by the disk and horns on a diadem, breaks through the panel containing the Carian text into the register above, obscuring the lower part of the dress and feet of the figure above, in a totally un-Egyptian fashion.[4] The lower wing masks the hind-quarters of the Apis. Iconographically, the goddess in this position could be Isis or Ḥathor. Descriptive labels, again empty in this scene and very crudely cut, would normally have identified the deities and the stela-owner.

This stela is wholly Egyptian in spirit, but totally alien in execution. It was certainly the product of a foreign sculptor, probably a Carian. There is nothing to suggest that the empty labels were intended in this particular monument to be inscribed in hieroglyphic by an Egyptian craftsman. Rather the stela was based on a common Egyptian prototype, some elements of which were not wholly understood by the foreign sculptor. No details of physiognomy are rendered in the figures, and the whole conception is maladroit, displaying solecisms that would never have been tolerated in an Egyptian workshop. Noteworthy are the summary outlines of the faces, the form of the sceptre of Osiris, the backward tilt of the head of the worshipper in the bottom register, and the plinth supporting the figure of the bull, which is so badly drawn that the back legs of the Apis are at a higher level than those at the front.

7. H5–1345   Plates VI; XXXV, 1

The inscribed surface of this rectangular limestone stela is intact. The top right-hand corner is broken away. Both the Carian (see p. 25 above) and the hieroglyphic inscriptions are boldly and deeply incised, and are evidently contemporary. They combine to complete the full height of the stela.

The hieroglyphic inscription, below the Carian, was never completed by the sculptor. It consists of one vertical column with the beginning of another, and reads:

Irš(ʒ) sʒ Nrskr sʒ Iʿḥ- . . .
'Iresh(a) son of Nerseker son of Iaḥ- . . .'

---

[1] Cf. **1**.
[2] Cf. **4, 5, 5a**.
[3] Cf. **1, 4, 5, 5a**, the first inscribed for the Apis.

[4] Egyptian sculptors do, however, occasionally break away from the discipline of the artistic canon, but not usually in such a dramatic manner as this.

As regards the reading of the Egyptian text, 𓈖𓄿 obviously stands for 𓈖𓄿. The name *Ỉrš(ꜣ)*[1] is not cited in Ranke, *Personennamen*, and is apparently foreign. It recalls the place-name 𓈖𓄿𓏏𓍯𓄿�ͤ, a region of Syria, named in the list of Tuthmosis III at Karnak.[2] No determinative is written after this name, but the two following filiations (*sꜣ*) prove that personal names are involved. The second name likewise is not known from Egyptian sources. The reading of the sign 𓄿 in this name as the vulture *nr* rather than *mwt* seems to be proved by the presence of the alphabetic signs *n* and *r* on either side of it. The seated-man determinative is present in this instance.

At the head of the second column the word *sꜣ*, 'son', is written, but without the downstroke[3] which correctly appears in the writing in column 1. The reading of the third name depends on the identification of the initial sign, possibly unfinished, with which it is written. Several possibilities are open, the most convincing of which is the crescent moon ⌢, *iꜥḥ* (Gardiner, *Egyptian Grammar*[3], Sign-list N 12[4]). The sign could also be interpreted as the rib ⌢, *spr* (Gardiner F 42).[5] Two other rare signs which have to be considered are the upper lip and teeth ⌢, in *spt*, 'lip' (Gardiner D 24), and the palm of the hand ⌢, *šsp*, used in the measure of a 'palm' (Gardiner N 11). Both seem unlikely candidates as elements of personal names.

As regards the language of the hieroglyphic inscription, it is tempting to suppose that this is Carian, and that the three names on the stela are those of Carians from the Memphite area. Support for this is found in the fact that the two personal names fully written out are foreign rather than Egyptian.[6] As group-writings 𓈖𓄿 and ⌢𓄿⌢ would be appropriate to foreign names. The final name, if it does begin with *Iꜥḥ*, could conceivably be Egyptian,[7] but since the name was left incomplete it is idle to speculate.

To judge from the structure of the three lines in the Carian text, three Carian names likewise could be present. There appears to be no correspondence, however, between the hieroglyphic and the Carian, as conventionally transliterated.

The cutting of the signs shows considerable skill, and both scripts may have been the work of a native Egyptian craftsman.

---

[1] J. R. Baines suggested to H. S. Smith that this name might be identical with that on **1**, see p. 59 above.

[2] Gauthier, *Dictionnaire géographique*, i, 97.

[3] Not infrequently absent in Egyptian texts.

[4] The word *ꜣbd* (late *ꜣbt*), 'month' (Gardiner N 11) is usually written without the rim within the crescent. It seems an unlikely element in a personal name, whereas *iꜥḥ* is frequently attested.

[5] A name *Spr(·i)-r-ꜥnḫ* is cited for the Old Kingdom in Ranke, op. cit. i, 306, 13.

[6] It may be remarked, however, that the second name could be rendered 'Terror of Sokar', but this seems dubious.

[7] For names beginning thus cf. Ranke, op. cit. i, 12–13, ii, 261.

APPENDICE I

La stèle carienne d'Abousîr

DURANT les fouilles dirigées par Borchardt à Abousîr, au nord-ouest de Saqqâra, une stèle funéraire, décorée d'une scène de *prothesis*, avait été découverte;[1] elle est conservée dans les musées de Berlin-Est, section d'égyptologie, inv. 19553 (24139); ici pl. XXX. Cette pièce a été considérée par les premiers commentateurs comme de facture grecque, ce jugement étant renforcé par la présence à droite, parallèlement au rebord extérieur, d'une inscription difficile à lire, mais regardée comme grecque; il s'agirait d'une légende archaïque du VIIe siècle,[2] reprise comme *Sammelbuch* 5121, *a* et *b*.[3]

Or, une nouvelle étude du relief lui-même, menée par R. V. Nicholls à propos des stèles de Saqqâra-Nord, ci-dessus, IIe partie, **3**, a montré que ce monument se rapproche beaucoup des objets publiés ici. La question s'est alors posée de savoir si l'inscription serait véritablement grecque, et attribuable au milieu des Hellénomemphites, à l'époque archaïque.[4] En fait, Miss L. H. Jeffery, interrogée la première sur ce point, avait émis l'opinion que la légende pourrait être *carienne* plutôt que grecque.[5]

Je crois aussi qu'on a affaire à une légende carienne, malheureusement très peu lisible. Les érudits allemands avaient essayé de retrouver du grec, avec une ligne disposée ainsi: lettres dont le sommet regarde la *droite* de la stèle, ligne commençant *en bas* à droite, se terminant en haut, donc sinistroverse. En réalité, on reconnaît quelques lettres cariennes typiques en lisant la ligne autrement: lettres dont le sommet regarde la *gauche* de la stèle, légende commençant *en haut* à droite, se terminant en bas, donc sinistroverse (cf. la stèle de Lausanne, plus loin). On aurait donc le schéma suivant:

Le premier mot commence par *u*; ensuite, zone illisible, puis séquence *m-u*, avec un *m* carien typique; plus loin, peut-être *u-n*, plus loin encore *n-u*; le dernier signe est certainement Φ, *25*, donc une finale spécifiquement carienne en -*25* (§ 13).

---

[1] L. Borchardt, *Das Grabdenkmal des Königs S'aḥu-reʿ*, i, Leipzig (1910), p. 135–137, fig. 187. Le commentaire est dû à R. Zahn, qui avait consulté pour l'inscription Hiller von Gaertringen et Wilamowitz. Bibliographie ci-dessus, p. 64.

[2] Op. cit., p. 137, avec diverses hésitations. Hiller proposait de retrouver l'épitaphe d'une Milésienne, nommée Stephanion: [Στεφ]ανίο[υ σᾶ]μα Μιλεσία[ς] (*sic*); Wilamowitz songeait à l'épitaphe d'un Phanis: Ἐπ[ὶ] Φάνιδ[ι ἐ]μ[ὶ] Αἰνεσία.

[3] Ce qui correspond aux lectures de Hiller et Wilamowitz,

respectivement. On en retrouve la trace dans le *Namenbuch* de Preisigke (1922), aux articles suivants: Αἰνεσία, Στεφάνιον, Φάνις. Ces trois rubriques sont désormais à supprimer, puisque la légende est à lire comme du carien: O. Masson, *ZPE* 23 (1976), p. 262.

[4] Voir ultérieurement J. Boardman, *The Greeks Overseas*, 1964, p. 152–153; M. M. Austin, *Greece and Egypt in the Archaic Age*, 1970, p. 57.

[5] Lettre à R. V. Nicholls (mai 1975), voir p. 64 n. 2.

APPENDICE II

Remarques sur la stèle de Lausanne

Sur la stèle, bien connue, de Lausanne, 46 F = **F** M–Y, l'inscription est disposée sur la marge extérieure droite de la pierre, de la même façon qu'à Abousîr, avec des lettres dont le sommet regarde la *gauche* de la stèle. A la suite d'une révision effectuée sur l'original[1] et de quelques réflexions, je propose aujourd'hui la lecture suivante:

m-s-n-r̦-29-32-k-27-e-14-25 | u-27 | k-a-v-e-a-25 | 25-u-33-7-e-th | s-a-v-a

Au début, il faut certainement distinguer, malgré l'absence de barre de séparation, deux mots, dont le premier sera *m-s-n-r-29*. Les s. 1 à 3 sont clairs. Pour le s. 4, il est désormais nécessaire, après les observations de V. Ševoroškin,[2] de renoncer à une lettre de forme et de valeur '*b*',[3] pour reconnaître une graphie de *15*, soit un *r* à panse tournée vers la droite. Ensuite, le signe *29*, en forme de *delta* renversé, mais ouvert en bas. Le mot obtenu est alors susceptible d'être comparé avec un mot d'Abou Simbel, 74 Š, écrit *m-e-s-n-a-r-29*; voir, en outre, le commentaire de **50**, 2.

Ensuite: le s. 6 est certainement *32*, en forme de E couché; pas d'hésitation pour 7 et 8. Le s. 9 est certainement un *e* (de dessin presque ovale) et le s. 11 ne peut être que ⊕, *25*; la lecture 'corrigée' de Zauzich,[4] avec *38-14-th* (*sic*), qui était proposée pour obtenir une séquence '*n-ī-th*' 'Neith' est donc exclue.

Plus loin, entre deux barres verticales nettes, une brève séquence, s. 12–13, avec un *u* évident, puis un signe difficile, ordinairement considéré comme un *e* maladroit (?). Une autre interprétation consisterait à voir ici une graphie très gauche de *27*, le signe en forme de carré (dessin correct au s. 8!). En effet, la présence d'un élément postposé *u-27* (voir § 12, 2) expliquerait l'emploi des barres verticales; en outre, on retrouverait une séquence finale du type *25-u-27*, comme dans **20**, **34**, etc., et sur la stèle D M–Y.

Pour l'avant-dernier mot, il y a seulement à remarquer la présence des deux *a* en forme de delta incliné. S. 20 à 25, lecture évidente; le s. 25 est un *th* (variation avec la stèle C M–Y, où le dernier signe est *25*). S. 26 à 29, lecture assurée, bien qu'il ne subsiste que le haut de 27 et 28; ici encore, deux *a* de même dessin que plus haut.

[1] Faite à Lausanne, Musée Historique Cantonal, grâce à l'aimable collaboration de M. Pierre Ducrey, professeur à l'Université de Lausanne (juin 1974).

[2] *RHA*, 1964, p. 41; *Issledovanija*, passim, et p. 309 (no. 14), p. 331 (index s.v. *msnr*).

[3] Il convient donc de rectifier sur ce point les éditions antérieures, et surtout Masson-Yoyotte, *Objets*, p. 24–25, 66 et 67; dans la fig. 29, le s. 2 est à supprimer. Pour les rares apparitions d'un signe de forme B en carien d'Égypte (Hou et Silsile), voir § 8, pour le signe *2*.

[4] Zauzich, p. 13–14.

CONCORDANCE OF NUMBERS

I. SAQQÂRA

Text no.	Excavator's no.	Antiquities Service Register no.	Plate no.	Location
1	H5-1349	3147	I, II, XXXI	Saqqâra
2	H5-1703+1006	3653+2758	I, XXXI	Saqqâra
3	H5-1229	2981	II, III, XXXII	Cambridge
4	H5-1343	3141	IV, XXXIII	B.M.
5	H5-1228	2980	V, XXXIII	Saqqâra
5a	H5-1223	2975	V, XXXIV	Cairo
6	H5-1222	2974	IV, XXXIV	Saqqâra
7	H5-1345	3143	VI, XXXV	Cairo
8	H5-1014	2776	VII, XXXV	Cairo
9	H5-1224	2976	VII, XXXV	B.M.
10	H5-1225	2977	VIII, XXXV	Cairo
11	H5-1404	3202	VIII	U.C.L.
12	H5-1344	3142	IX	Cairo
13	H5-1347	3145	IX, XXXVI	Cairo
13a	H5-1348	3146		U.C.L.
14	H5-1350	3148	X	Cambridge
15	H5-1351	3149	X	B.M.
16	H5-1352	3150	XI	Cambridge
17	H5-1353	3151	XI	Cairo
18	H5-1354	3152	XII	B.M.
19	H5-1355	3153	XII	Oxford
20	H5-1356	3154	XIII, XXXVI	Cairo
21	H5-1357	3155	XIII	Cairo
22	H5-1358	3156	XIV	Cairo
23	H5-1359	3157	XIV	Cairo
24	H5-1360	3158	XV	Birmingham
25	H5-1361	3159	XV	Cairo
26	H5-1362	3160	XVI, XXXVI	Cairo
27	H5-1401	3199	XVI	Cairo
28	H5-1434	3232	XVII	Cairo
29	H5-1435	3237	XVII	Cairo
30	H5-1440	3238	XVIII	Oxford
31	H5-1501	3299	XVIII	B.M.
32	H5-1506+H6-374	3304	XIX	Durham+Saqqâra
33	H5-1507	3305+2446	XIX	Cairo
34	H5-1832	3782	XX, XXXVI	Cairo
35	H5-1833	3783	XX	Cairo
36	H5-1872	3834	XXI, XXXVII	Cairo
37	H5-1873	3835	XXI	U.C.L.
38	H5-1980	3984	XXII	U.C.L.
39	H5-1346	3144	XXIII, XXXVII	B.M.
40	H6-418	2517	XXIII, XXXVII	U.C.L.
41	H5-1565	3394	XXIII	Saqqâra
42	Inscr. 10 *in situ*		XXXVII	Saqqâra
43	H5-1819	3969	XXIV, XXXVII	B.M.
44	H5-1504	3302	XXIV	B.M.
45	H5-353	1025	XXIV	Cambridge
45a	H6-372	2444	XXV	B.M.
46	H6-373	2445	XXV	B.M.
47	H5-1505	3303	XXV	B.M.
47a	H5-1503	3301	XXVI	B.M.
47b	H6-386	2462	XXVI	B.M.
48	H5-2432	4637	XXVI	B.M.
48a	H5-35	687	XXVI	Saqqâra
48b	S 72/3-42	6028		Saqqâra

Text no.	Excavator's no.	Antiquities Service Register no.	Plate no.	Location
48c	S 72/3–39	6025		Saqqâra
48d	S 74/5–20	6232	XXVI	Saqqâra
49	S 75/6–24	6387		Saqqâra

II. BUHEN

Text no.	Archaeological reference	Plate no.	Location
50	Inv. 1616 (K.11.4)	XXVII, XXXVIII	Khartoum
51	Graffito 66F on pilaster 18 of Temple	XXVII, XXXVIII	Khartoum
52	Graffito 68F on door-jamb 20 of Temple	XXVIII	Khartoum
53	Graffito 69F		Unknown
54	Graffito 70F		Unknown
55	Graffito 67F on column 31 of Temple	XXVIII, XXIX	Khartoum

III. SAQQÂRA

Monuments, possibly Carian, not included in this volume

Excavator's no.	Antiquities Service Register no.	Location	Notes
H5–186	838	Durham, Gulbenkian Museum no. 1971.139	No inscription
H6–389	2465	Saqqâra	
H5–1368	3166	B.M. 67249	Obscure signs, possibly not Carian
H5–1502	3300	B.M. 67253–4	Two fragments; no inscription
H5–1843	3793	B.M. 67237	No inscription
S 75/6–28	6392	Saqqâra	See p. 49 n. 1

INDEXES

I. CARIAN INDEXES

A. INDEX OF THE SAQQÂRA AND BUHEN INSCRIPTIONS

i. *Normal Index*

NOTE: References are given by text

a-d-o-s-h-a-v-k-o-s, **37**
a-k-29-43-u-r, **50**; *a-k-29-?-u-r*, **51**
a-m-n-27-k, **36**
a-m-?-?-?-32-s, **15**
a-ṣ-[, **1**
a-v-d-e-o-n-25, **35**
a-v-[d]-e-r, **50**; *a-v-ḍ-e-r*, **51**
a-v-d-e-r-25, **7**; **43**
a-v-d-e-r-25: *u-m-27*, **1**
a-v-d-38-ọ, **1**
a-v-e-?-25-h-e-o-27-g, **30**
?/a-v-g-é-l-é-v-25, **44**
a-v-h-e-d-a-25, **31**
a-v-th-u-th-25, **36**
a-v-th-u-th-25-h-e, **35**
a-v-14-a-é-25: *u-m-27*, **14**
a-v-38-o-n-25: *u-27*, **34**
a-25-v-25, **55**
a-?-?-e-29-a-v-ṇ-25-h-e, **15**

d-o-u-l-ạ-32, **41**
d-28-h-s-e-25 | *u-m-27*, **35**
d-30-o-v-25-h-38, **28**

e-a-v-29-[, **47**
e-é-v-s-e-25, **53**
e-g-é-27-s-25, **48d**
e-g-n-k-s, **25 a, b**
e-g-n-u-o-k-25-h-e, **10b**
e-v-o-32, **6**; **8**
e-v-o-32-25, **19**
e-14-u-v-o-32-25, **24**

é-e-a-s-e-?-?/?, **17**
é-e-25-h-l-e-29-s-h-e-25, **38**
é-k-27-n-o-v-e-25, **21**
é-38, **1**

g-32-25-o-7-25, **27**

h-e-27-k, **24**

k-e-th-a-u-25, **10a**
k-14-o-d (ou *30?*)-*v-e-s*, **27**

m-a-v-a-e-43-v-27-7-25-h-e, **39**
m-a-v-m-27-é-n-25-h-e, **17**
m-d-ṭh-o, **32**
m-e-d-v-n-25-h-e, **32**
m-e-29-a-v-n-25, **6**
ṃ-e-29-v-a-25-h-e, **8**

m-g̣-14-ọ-n-25, **51**
m-g-[, **49**
m-h-s-e-n-14-25-h-e, **42**
m-k-d-31-25-32-d, **41**
m-k-u-25-o-7, **11**
m-k-14-n-u-k-25-h-e, **20**
m-s-e-29-v-o-ḳ [? *u-27*, **43**
m-s-n-a-[, **46**
m-s-n-a-25-n, **53**; **54**
m-s-n-a-25-u-25, **50**
m-s-t-28-n-?-25, **19**
m-u-k-32-25-o-7-25, **13**
m-u-o-27-25, **55**
m-7-27-th-25-h-e, **22**
m-14-k-u-m-e, **10a**
m-14-14-u-25, **19**
m-38-a-l-v-n, **4**
m-?-u-?-e-25/?, **2**

n-[, **4**
n-é-v-27-25-h-e, **25 a, b**
n-g-[, **44**
n-g-a-é-k-h-e, **10b**; **25a**
n-g-a-28-k, **3**; **9**
n-k-[, **39**
n-k-o-25, **2**; **8**; **19**; **31**
n-k-o-25-h-e, **35**
n-s-k-o-v-e-25, **40**
n-v-s-e-25, **18**
ṇ-v-s-3̣8-[, **45a**
n-27-42-25, **26**
n-32-g-o-k-25, **21**
n-32-g-o-k-25-h-e, **4**; **5**; **8**; **12**; **20**; **23**; **24**; **27**; **32**; **34**; **38**
n-32-g-o-u-25, **6**
n-32-s-a-14-25: *h-e*, **34**
n-32-14-o-k-25-h-e, **36**

?/r-a-é-v-e-th, **17**
r-a-n-s-th-e-[?, **16**
r-a-v-k-a-e-25-u-m-27, **9**
r-a-v-u-25-o-7, **22**
r-g-40-a-14-25 | *u-m-a*, **5**
r-v-32-d-e-25-h-e, **12**
r-27-k-u-v-14, **42**
r-28-e-k-25 | *u-m-27*, **30**

s-a-k-u-th-25 | *u-27*, **20**
s-e-v-a-d, **41**
s-o-n-k-27-25, **13**; **26**

95

ii. *Reverse Index*

NOTE: Entries are arranged in order according to the last letter of each word

Afin de faciliter les comparaisons avec le vocabulaire de Saqqâra et de Bouhen, on a rassemblé ici, avec la nouvelle transcription utilisée dans cet ouvrage, les mots qui figurent dans les autres documents cariens d'Égypte, soit:

a. Objets pharaoniques = Ob., plus lettre, d'après l'édition Masson–Yoyotte, *Objets*, mais avec certaines modifications.

b. Graffites d'Abydos = Ab. 1 F, etc., ou 1 Y, etc.; dans la mesure du possible, on a utilisé ici les révisions faites par J. Yoyotte en 1955 et ajouté les principaux inédits réunis par lui, cités 1 Y, etc.

c. Graffites de Thèbes (tombeau de Montouemhat) = Th. 47 Š, etc.; graffites cités et le plus souvent lus d'après l'édition provisoire de Ševoroškin, *Issledovanija*, p. 310 et 314–315 (cf. *RHA* 1964, p. 42–43); certaines lectures ont été modifiées d'après les photographies communiquées par J. Leclant.[1]

d. Graffites de Silsile = Si. 53 F, etc.; ces graffites n'ont pas été revus et demeurent difficiles; on doit les citer d'après les copies anciennes, recueillies chez Friedrich; quelques améliorations chez Ševoroškin, *Issledovanija*, p. 310 et 315 (cf. *RHA* 1964, p. 43); notamment, 53 F à lire dextroverse.

e. Graffites d'Abou-Simbel = AS 72 Š, etc.; textes revus et complétés par A. Bernand et A. Ali en 1956, avec édition donnée par Ševoroškin, *Issledovanija*, p. 310–311 et 316 (cf. *RHA* 1964, p. 43–44).

f. Graffite du Gebel Sheikh Suleiman = GSS 72 F; pour ce graffite isolé, jamais photographié, on dispose essentiellement d'une copie de Sayce.[2]

g. Bronze de Léningrad = Léningrad 4 Š. Statuette inscrite publiée par Ševoroškin, *RHA* 1964, p. 57–65.

h. Lion de bronze = Lion. Statuette inscrite publiée par O. Masson, *Kadmos* 15 (1976), p. 82–83.[3]

i. *Normal Index*

a-l-v-th-h-[?, Ab. 9 F
a-o-v-[, Ob. A
a-v-d-e-r, Ab. 18 F
a-v-k-a-38-s, Léningrad 4 Š
a-v-n-o-k-h-e, Ob. Ka
a-40-14-28-v-e-25, Ab. 19 F

ḏ-e-u-l-[*a*]*-35-e-25*, Ob. A
ḏ-u-g-14-u-l-ạ, Th. 55 Š
?/*d-29-o-th-n-s*, Th. 59 Š
d-30-o-v-25, Ob. B

e-a-d-7-e, Ab. 27 Y
e-k-u-14-25, Ab. 13a F
e-o-k-27-7-25, Ob. a (50 F)
e-s-o-v-25-h-e, Ob. C
e-s-28-v-38-27-14, Si. 53 F
e-v-a-s-ạ, Si. 54 F
e-v-a-v-s-e-25, Ab. 2b F
e-28-30-v-25, AS 76 Š
ẹ-é-s-n-14-25-ọ-t-a-[, Ab. 21 F

g-l-e-30-s, Th. 60 Š
g-o-29-n-n-m-25-k-ọ-s/?, Th. 50 Š
g-v-[, Si. 57 F
g-14-28-l-v, Th. 48; 51 Š

h-a-é-27, Ab. 26a F
h-a-v-v-25, Ab. 26b F
h-e-ḳ-u-14-14-a-n-o-s-e, Ab. 14 F
h-e-th-u-p, Si. 39 F
h-?-u-v-l-25, Ab. 8 Y

k-a-th, Si. 53 F
k-a-v-e-a-25, Ob. F
k-a-35-h-e-h, AS 78 Š
k-e-g-25-30-u-s-a-s, AS 79 Š
k-m-v-d-33-s-n-27, AS 75 Š

k-m-v-o-s-k-25, Ab. 11 F
k-o-v-o-s, Lion
?/*k-u-n-31-a-k-27*, Lion
k-u-o-7-ḥ-[, Ob. E
k-25-k-?-s-r, GSS 72 F
k-?-27-a-30-v-k-ạ-ḳ-ḷ, Si. 54 F

l-e-31-25-d-27-n-s-a, Ab. 25 F
l-e-38-25-25-ṃ-27, Si. 59 F
l-s-e-s, Ab. 25 F
l-27-l-k, Th. 52 Š
l-27-25-ọ-7, Ab. 17 F
l-27-40-30-v-th-e-14-[, Si. 56 F
l-28-ḷ-e-ḳ-14, AS 78 Š
l-28-r, AS 78 Š
l-28-14-a-ṛ, Si. 57 F
?/*l-32-ṇ-ḳ-k-m-28*, Th. 50 Š

m-a-d-s-25, Ab. 5a, b, c F
m-a-k-27-38, Ab. 2a F
m-a-v-a-27-é-n, Ob. Ka
m-a-v-n-a-25-25-h-e, Ob. G
m-a-v-8-27-é-n, Ob. Kb
m-a-v-25-ọ-ḏ-o-u, AS 72 Š
ṃ-a-v-28-g-h-25, GSS 72 F
m-a-?-e-k-?-14-25, Ab. 12 F
m-d-a-14, Th. 49 Š
m-e-s-e-v-e, Ab. 1 F
m-e-s-n-a-r-29, AS 74 Š
m-e-s-n-a-25-30, AS 78 Š
m-ẹ-u-n-28-35, Ab. 6 F
m-e-27-32, Ab. 15 Y
m-e-29-v-27-25-u-27, Ob. D
m-g-k-27-38/?, Ob. M
m-g-u-l-a, Ob. b (65 F)
m-g-u-l-e-25, Ab. 4 F
m-g-u-l-14-35-ọ-v-25, Ab. 10 F
m-k-é-v-e-25-ṿ-u, AS 76 Š

[1] J'ai utilisé aussi une documentation prise sur place, durant une visite du monument (octobre 1975). Une publication spéciale est en préparation.

[2] Voir ci-dessus, commentaire de **22** et de **30**.

[3] On n'a pas recueilli dans cet index les documents suivants: ostrakon de Hou (38 F); graffites d'Abou-Simbel qui sont en réalité grecs (33 et 36 F); divers douteux (49 et 52 F).

ii. *Reverse Index*

NOTE: Entries are arranged in order according to the last letter of each word

?/s-th-d-a
]-a-d-7-e-a
v-25-o-29-a-h-a
m-g-u-l-a
ḍ-u-g-14-u-l-ạ
?/o-v-r-a/?
e-v-a-s-ạ
l-e-31-25-d-27-n-s-a
ẹ́-ẹ́-s-n-14-25-ọ-t-a-[
?-l-27-h-30-31-?-ṭ-a
s-a-v-a

th-32-s-a-ḍ
ṛ-a-l-p-a-e-30-a-d

a-v-n-o-k-h-e
29-d-o-v-u-7-h-e
?/14-th-28-v-e-25-h-e
e-s-o-v-25-h-e
m-a-v-n-a-25-25-h-e
s-d-a-28-25-h-e
h-e-ḳ-u-14-14-a-n-o-s-e
14-v-n-o-s-e
m-e-s-e-v-e
]-m-v-e
e-a-d-7-e

k-a-35-h-e-h
a-l-v-th-h-[?
k-u-o-7-ḥ-[

l-27-l-k
14-u-n-k
s-th-d-u-n-e-p-u-k/?
31-27-k
32-g-32-k
r-a-?-?-e-25-v-32-k

k-?-27-a-30-v-k-ạ-ḳ-ḷ
th-o-v-l
?/o-32-g-o-32-k-l-?-l/?

m-a-v-a-27-ẹ́-n
m-a-v-8-27-ẹ́-n
r-a-v-30-l-e-o-n
m-s-28-r-a-e-k-e-th-ọ-n
30-r-n-n-ṣ-ṇ-[
n-28-th-u-p-27-n

?/th-14-l-d-o/?
s-l-m-o-d-o
u-k-14-v-e-ụ-a-k-14-v-m-ọ
r-a-n-o/?
28-k-?-n-o
n-a-v-a-v-ẹ-s-o-[

14-v-e-th-o
?/32-a-ẹ́-u-g-30-25-o/?

h-e-th-u-p

l-28-14-a-ṛ
a-v-d-e-ṛ
k-25-k-?-s-r
m-?-d-u-r
l-28-r
27-s-a-33-31-o-32-r
m-14-k-u-?-r
]-v-25-32-30-?-ṛ-[

m-v-37-e-g-a-s/?
k-e-g-25-30-u-s-a-s
34-v-a-s
l-s-e-s
?/d-29-o-th-n-s
g-o-29-n-n-m-25-k-ọ-s/?
s-l-r-a-th-l-o-s
n-th-a-l-29-27-32-d-27-th-ọ-r-o-s/?
28-k-s-n-s-o-s
k-o-v-o-s
p-n-o-2-l-th-s
?-a-v-s
 g̣-l-e-30-s
a-v-k-a-38-s

?/27-32-n-25-27-n-o-ṭ/?

k-a-th
30-th-25-l-a-th/?
25-u-33-7-e-th
ụ-?-?-?-ḷ-25-th
n-e-29-25-ṭh
]-u-?-?-th-40-38-th/?

u-30-s-n-u
m-a-v-25-ọ-ḍ-o-u
40-a-n-o-u
m-k-ẹ́-v-e-25-v-u
?/th-29-u-[?

30-25-a-14-28-l-v
g-14-28-l-v
a-o-v-[

u-25-o-7
r-a-v-u-25-o-7
l-27-25-ọ-7

m-d-a-14
n-m-d-ạ-14

Note: References are to pages

PLATE I

1. **1**, inscribed part (pp. 20, 58 ff.)

2. **2** (pp. 21, 60)

PLATE II

2. 3 (pp. 22, 61 ff.)

1. 1 (pp. 20, 58 ff.)

PLATE III

3; partial view showing inscribed right margin (pp. 22, 61 ff.)

PLATE IV

2. 6 (pp. 24 f., 85 f.)

1. 4 (pp. 22 f., 70 ff.)

PLATE V

2. 5a (pp. 24, 83 ff.)

1. 5 (pp. 23 f., 79 ff.)

PLATE VI

7 (pp. 25 f., 86 f.)

PLATE VII

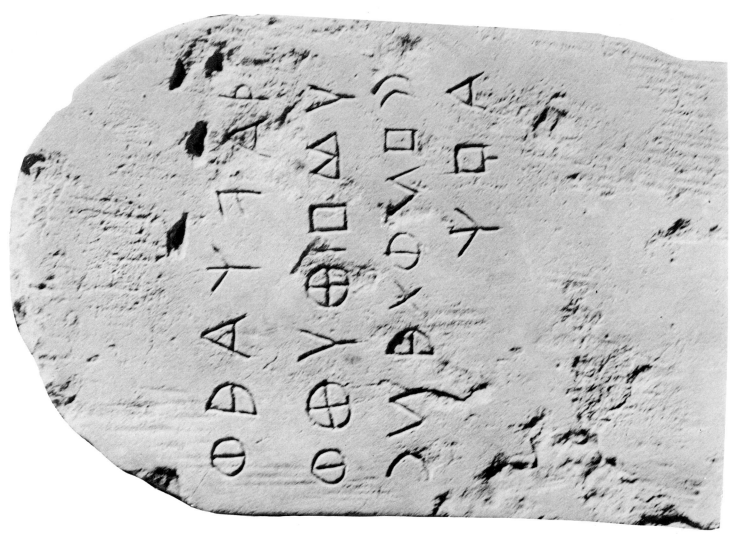

PLATE VIII

2. **11** (p. 29)

1. **10** (pp. 27 ff.)

PLATE IX

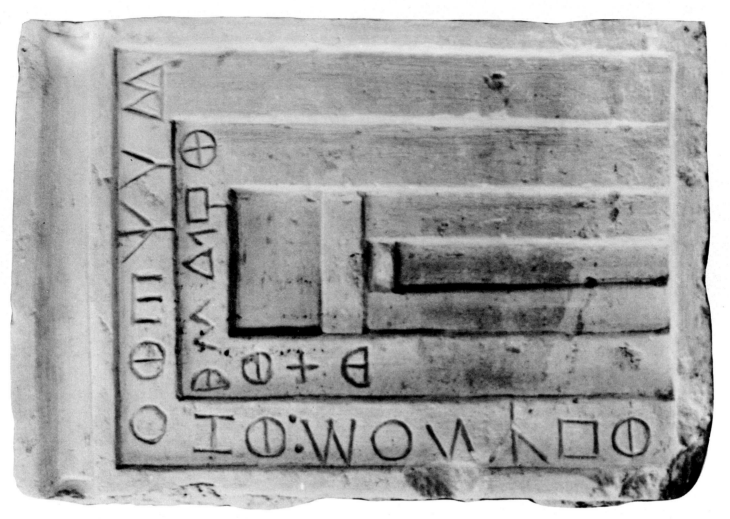

2. 13 (pp. 29 f.)

1. 12 (p. 29)

PLATE X

2. **15** (pp. 30 f.)

1. **14** (p. 30)

PLATE XI

2. 17 (pp. 31 f.)

1. 16 (p. 31)

PLATE XII

2. **19** (p. 33)

1. **18** (p. 32)

PLATE XIII

2. **21** (p. 34)

1. **20** (pp. 33 f.)

PLATE XIV

2. **23** (p. 35)

1. **22** (pp. 34 f.)

PLATE XV

2. 25 (p. 36)

1. 24 (pp. 35 f.)

PLATE XVI

2. **27** (p. 37)

1. **26** (p. 36)

PLATE XVII

2. 29 (p. 38)

1. 28 (pp. 37 f.)

PLATE XVIII

2. **31** (pp. 39 f.)

1. **30** (p. 39)

PLATE XIX

2. 33 (p. 40)

1. 32 (p. 4c)

PLATE XX

2. 35 (pp. 41 f.)

1. 34 (p. 41)

PLATE XXI

2. **37** (pp. 42 f.)

1. **36** (p. 42)

PLATE XXII

1. **38** (p. 43)

1. **38**, detail with inscription (p. 43)

PLATE XXIII

1. **39** (pp. 43 f.)

2. **40** (pp. 44 f.)

3. **41** (p. 45)

PLATE XXIV

1. **43** (p. 46)

2. **44** (pp. 46 f.)

3. **45** (p. 47)

PLATE XXV

1. **45a** (p. 47)

2. **46** (pp. 47 f.)

3. **47** (p. 48)

PLATE XXVI

1. **47a** (p. 48)

3. **48** (p. 48)

2. **47b** (p. 48)

4. **48a** (p. 48)

5. **48d** (p. 49)

PLATE XXVII

1. **50** (pp. 50 f.)

2. **51** (pp. 51 f.)

PLATE XXVIII

1. **52** (p. 53)

2. **55** (pp. 53 f.)

PLATE XXIX

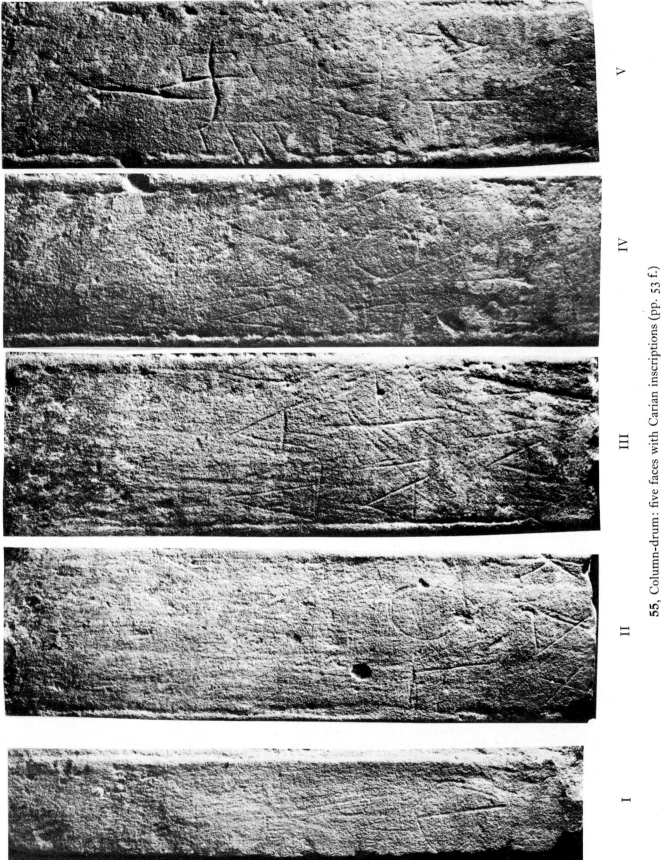

55, Column-drum: five faces with Carian inscriptions (pp. 53 f.)

V

IV

III

II

I

PLATE XXX

Stela of Abûsîr (Berlin 19553)
(photo by courtesy of the Staatliche Museen zu Berlin)

PLATE XXXI

1. **1** (pp. 20, 58 ff.)

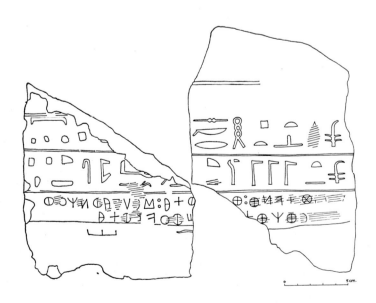

2. **2** (pp. 21, 60)

PLATE XXXII

3 (pp. 22, 61 ff.)

PLATE XXXIII

2. 5 (pp. 23 f., 79 ff.)

1. 4 (pp. 22 f., 70 ff.)

PLATE XXXIV

2. **6** (pp. 24 f., 85 f.)

1. **5a** (pp. 24, 83 ff.)

PLATE XXXV

1. **7** (pp. 25 f., 86 f.)

2. **8** (pp. 26 f.)

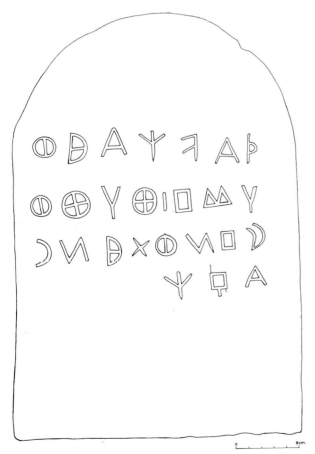

3. **9** (p. 27)

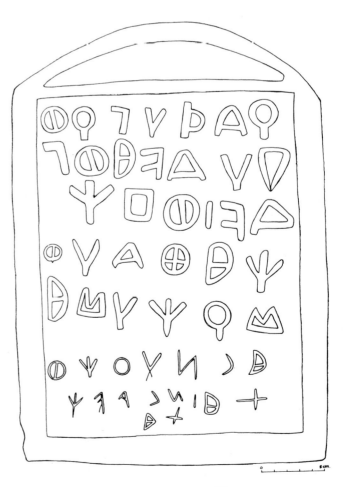

4. **10** (pp. 27 ff.)

PLATE XXXVI

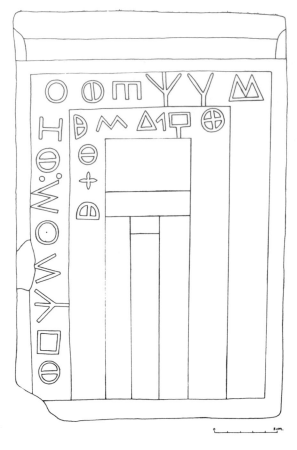

1. **13** (pp. 29 f.)

2. **20** (pp. 33 f.)

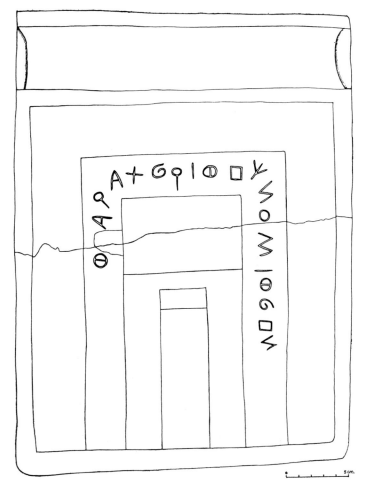

3. **26** (p. 36)

4. **34** (p. 41)

PLATE XXXVII

1. **36** (p. 42)

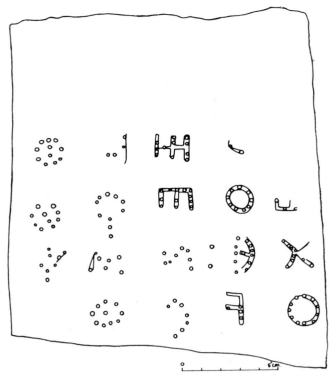

3. **40** (pp. 44 f.)

2. **39** (pp. 43 f.)

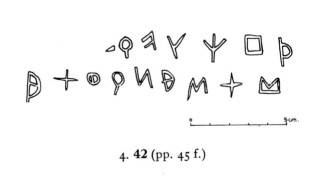

4. **42** (pp. 45 f.)

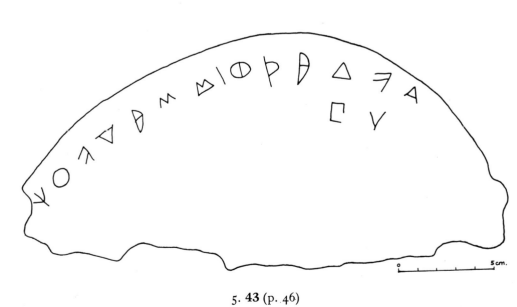

5. **43** (p. 46)

PLATE XXXVIII

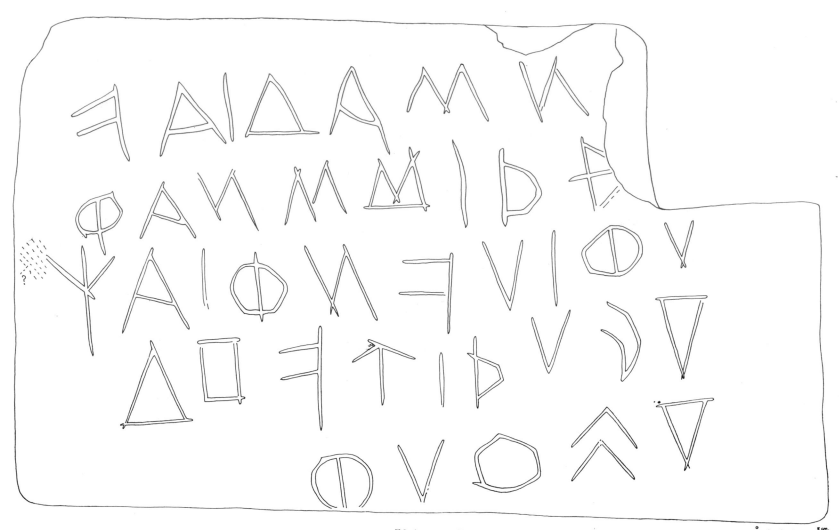

1. **50** (pp. 50 f.)

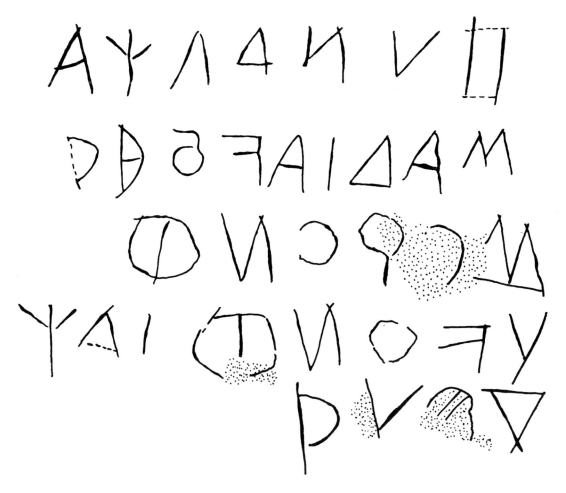

2. **51** (pp. 51 f.)